Advance Pr.

"If Michael Menzies isn't the love-child of Noël Coward and Marlene Dietrich, he should be. *Deeply Superficial* is first-class all the way."

—Dana Delaney, actress

"*Deeply Superficial* must exist by every bedside like a midnight snack that is so delicious it is impossible to put down."

—Robby Benson, actor/director

"What would you do with a pot de crème of a book consisting of a dollop of Gore Vidal's delicious sarcasm, a soupcon of Orphan Annie gamin joy of life, a pinch of Oprah Winfrey's exhilarating enthusiasm, and one sprinkle of your favorite gossip columnist's relish for the dirt. If you drool at the ingredients, rush, rush to get Michael Menzies tantalizing memoir."

—Pat Carroll, actress

"Charming, touching, funny, it's a joy to read."

—Stephen Lloyd, producer and writer,
How I Met Your Mother

"A gift of expression that makes one wish to fly freely into what we are and what we might be."

—Michele Lee, actress and singer

"Real? Made up? Who cares! Michael Menzies has willed his dreams to come true. The book is as magical as Michael himself. Bravo!"

—Bud Cort, actor and director

"Michael Menzies is a charming and talented man and has written a charming and talented memoir of his notable life in the arts."

—André Bishop, Artistic Director,
Lincoln Center Theater

"Michael's book turns a phrase with the same delight as his life does. His stories are funny and his voice is true."

—Raffaella de Laurentiis, film producer

"A heady mixture of innocence and sophistication—I loved it."

—Fenella Fielding, actress

DEEPLY SUPERFICIAL
Noël Coward, Marlene Dietrich, and Me

Michael Menzies

For Eduardo

CONTENTS

CHAPTER ONE

Adoption

Despite the fact there is no documentary evidence to suggest, much less back up, my conviction that I was adopted, this did not stop me from approaching my parents with this firmly-held belief.

In November 1946 I was twelve years old, the second of four children born to Clive and Mary Menzies, a devoted middle-class couple who had lived their entire lives—single and married— in faraway New Zealand.

What finally brought about this discussion of adoption was the birthday gift of money my mother had given me with one proviso: I could only buy books. This and the toy theater that Clive had built for me remain the best remembered and most-loved of all the gifts I received during my childhood.

At that age I understood quantity better than quality and so I bought the biggest books that the money allowed me. Among these was the first autobiography written by Noël Coward called *Present Indicative*. The cover featured the author, elegantly suited and poised with his pen upraised, as if the photographer had interrupted his writing.

I proudly showed my mother the purchases I had made.

She liked *Tales from Shakespeare*. She had never heard of *Le Petit Prince* but didn't seem to mind it. "Seems charming," she said as she flicked through the pages. *Prater Violet* and *The Berlin Stories* by Christopher Isherwood elicited no response, but when she came to the Coward autobiography, she made a sort of gurgling sound, clutched her pearls, and quite clearly displayed disapproval.

"I don t think this is quite suitable," she said.

"But you said I could buy whatever I liked." (It was the largest book I had bought.)

"I did," she admitted, "but..." Her voice trailed off, her mouth a moue, full of lemon juice.

Of course, this made me extremely curious and I immediately read Coward's autobiography, gulping his words and thoughts greedily, as if they were English trifle (to this day, my favorite dessert). Like the character Amanda in Coward's masterpiece play *Private Lives,* I became "jagged with sophistication" at the age of twelve, and went around saying, "I love you awfully. Awfully, awfully, dreadfully, awfully."

I thought it sounded very worldly.

Reading between the lines of his book, I became aware that Coward was a homosexual. A reference concerning a vacation he took at age fifteen with an artist ten years his senior, who painted Noël nude posing on rocks at the beach, was the first indication. But as he gained adulthood, journeys undertaken with male companions only became commonplace and clinched the conviction.

I knew I was "different" at age five, when in the changing room at the school swimming pool I couldn't take my eyes off Barry Fenton's perfect legs. I wanted to touch them, tracing their outline, feeling their strength. I felt guilty and excited and terribly confused. I knew instinctively these feelings were "wrong." To this day a shapely male leg still can send shivers through me.

The knowledge that I shared these inclinations towards the male sex with Coward comforted me hugely. All the guilt and shame I had felt about this part of my nature growing up, and the resultant exclusion and avoidance of straight boyhood companions, slid from me like a snake shedding its skin.

After consuming *Present Indicative*, my sexuality never bothered me again.

I could become as beloved and famous and as successful as Coward, for his homosexuality never held him back. Although it was well known in most circles that he preferred the male sex, it was never discussed openly during his lifetime. He made no effort to hide it, but felt coming out may disappoint a "few blue haired old ladies in Groton-by-the-Sea who still fancy me. I wouldn't want to disillusion them."

I was determined that my homosexuality would not hold me back either. If Coward could do it, so could I.

I was deeply impressed by two remarks in his book. He refused to suffer, he wrote rather grandly. I thought this was an excellent philosophy, although a few chapters later he described days of pain and agony and even hospitalization from a case of hemorrhoids. But the maxim "refuse to suffer" entered and stayed in my consciousness.

The other remark that struck me with force was that he always traveled first class. I interpreted "first class" as a state of mind rather than what is written on the ticket.

Present Indicative had made an indelible impression upon me to say the least.

It was also through this book that I was introduced to Marlene Dietrich, the glamorous German actress/singer.

It appeared that she had seen Coward play the eponymous *Scoundrel* in a Hollywood film. Enormously taken with his elegance, his clipped speaking voice, and most of all his strong individual and very personal acting style, she felt compelled to phone him in England, where he resided, from her home in Los Angeles.

International calls at that time were difficult, handled by operators, and often sputtering with static.

Already world famous, Marlene Dietrich purred huskily into the overseas connection, "This is Marlene Dietrich."

"And I am Marie, Queen of Rumania," Coward replied, hanging up the telephone. He thought it was a practical joke being played on him by one of his friends. He would have none of it.

Further insistent calls convinced him it was indeed Dietrich, and their lifelong and devoted friendship began that day.

As for my book purchases, I didn't bother with *Tales from Shakespeare*, agreeing with Dame Edith Evans' opinion that Lady Macbeth had a "peculiar idea of hospitality." I gave *Le Petit Prince* to my sister, who scrawled all over it with crayons.

I liked the Isherwood books, but I loved Coward's!

So I re-read *Present Indicative*.

The more I read about both Noël and Marlene, scouring magazines for news of them, going to any movies that featured either of them that were shown in Auckland, New Zealand, listening almost exclusively to their music, the more I became convinced that in some way, somehow, sometime I was connected to them in a mysterious, inexplicable manner. I didn't fit in at school; I didn't fit in at home. I even told Barry Fenton that his legs were as beautiful as Marlene Dietrich's. He told me I was crazy and ran off.

And then—of course! A flash like a paparazzi camera—it all became clear: I was their love child (the dates didn't really fit but were close enough if one fudged a little). It could have happened. It could be true—I could be their offspring!

After dinner one night, with my brothers and sister outside playing some childish game that with my newfound sophistication I eschewed, I approached my parents.

It had taken a few days for me to build up the courage to do this. It could forever change our relationship and my life.

"I have something I want to tell you," I said. Mary laid aside her knitting (a Fair Isle sweater) and looked at me with kind interest. Clive stopped whatever he was doing and gave me his full attention.

Boldly and with total confidence, I spoke in a rush.

"I – know – I – am – adopted – and – I– know – my – real – parents – are – Noël – Coward – and – Marlene – Dietrich. I – also – know– the reason – they – sent – me – to – New – Zealand – was – to – avoid – an – international – scandal – which – could – have – ruined – their – careers!"

The words tumbled out like a waterfall, an avalanche.

"That's how I came to be here," I finished a little lamely. "In New Zealand," I added. I made New Zealand sound so strange, as if I were on the Moon.

It had always seemed to me very unfair that I was stuck in that country at the bottom of every map of the world, when I knew for a fact that I was meant to be up near the top of the map—striding the boulevards of Paris, jostling with opening night crowds, attending plays or films or personal appearances of my "real" parents. Sailing across the Atlantic on the *Bremen* or the *Normandie* or the *Queen Mary* (first class, of course).

Neither Clive nor Mary responded.

There was a long, awkward silence.

Clive eventually broke it.

"You are right, son," he said. "You are their child.

Just please don't tell your brothers and sister."

A weight lifted from my shoulders. All knots of doubt unraveled. I felt free! It was true: I was the love child of Coward and Dietrich.

I had never loved Clive or Mary more than at that moment.

Years later, I realized the enormous gift they had given me: the freedom to indulge my imagination, no matter how wild, how improbable. It was a better gift than the toy theater or the money they had given me to buy books. In fact, it was one of the greatest gifts I have ever been given, and it has shaped my life.

CHAPTER TWO

Deeply Superficial

It was pop artist Andy Warhol who coined the phrase.

"I am deeply superficial," he once admitted.

A flippant response or a serious one? I like to think he was serious.

Unlike Warhol, Noël Coward and Marlene Dietrich attempted to overcome the critical perception of them as "superficial." They would never have considered describing themselves as such, "deeply" or otherwise.

Coward's critics bemoaned the "thinness" of his plays. He briskly answered them: "Next time I will write you a fat one."

After the release of her first two films (*The Blue Angel* and *Morocco*), critics who had praised Dietrich's acting now focused instead on the seductive allure of her face, so perfectly lit, and the beauty of her legs, lauded as "the most beautiful legs in the world." However, they considered her lightweight, and seldom took her seriously as an actress. I believe this was a result of the choice of her material.

The lives of Coward and Dietrich are extraordinary by anyone's standards.

They both became internationally famous in the 1920s and remained so for the rest of their lives. They lived in the rarefied air of celebrity. They had created images in the public eye as glamorous, sophisticated, elegant, world-weary, mysterious, and wildly successful. They were world travelers. They dressed exquisitely.

7

They were witty. They were sought after.

In 1924, Noël wrote a "great whacking part" for himself in his breakthrough play, *The Vortex,* which had major success in London and New York. He played a drug-addicted son of a vain mother who had lovers the same age as he. This immediately established him as a "modern" writer/actor whose finger was on the pulse of the times. A chronicler of the Bright Young Things.

"Success took me to her bosom like a maternal boa constrictor," Coward wrote. "Decadent," "neurotic," "filth" answered some critics. It was all excellent for business and gave Coward a reputation as "smart," "nervy," and "brilliant," all of which would remain part of his legend for the next fifty years or so.

Because of the immense success of *The Vortex,* producers were clamoring for more from Noël, so he dug deep into his drawer and rescued a couple of comedies that had previously been roundly rejected by most theater managements. In no time flat he had three plays running simultaneously in the West End. *Hay Fever* and *Fallen Angels* joined *The Vortex* as long-running hits, sealing Noël's position in the theater.

He became a master of self-publicity. "The legend of my modesty grew and grew," he noted. "I became extraordinarily unspoiled by my great success!"

In 1930, Marlene Dietrich shot to worldwide fame with her first starring role in the German-made movie *The Blue Angel.* Paramount Pictures instantly signed her to a long-term Hollywood contract. She left straight from the premiere screening of her film in her native Berlin to catch the boat train and sail to America. No shilly-shallying for our Marlene!

The same year Noël wrote music, lyrics, and the book to his operetta *Bitter Sweet,* followed soon after by his masterpiece play *Private Lives.* He also wrote and staged the massive *Cavalcade,* a deeply patriotic play with a cast of four hundred. No shilly-shallying for Noël either! By the age of thirty-one, he was known throughout his profession as The Master.

He was constantly recognized, constantly quoted. Fodder for gossip magazines, his stories and quotes told and re-told at parties.

"Did you hear what Noël said...?"

"Do you mean the Douglas Fairbanks story?"

And someone would tell the story: "A woman dining in the same restaurant as Coward approached him and said, 'You must remember me. I met you when I was with Douglas Fairbanks.'"

"Madam," replied Noël, "there are days when I don't even remember Douglas Fairbanks."

Laughter would remind someone of another story...and so the legend began to grow. Was there anything he couldn't do?

"Well, I can't saw ladies in half, or perform on the trapeze, but I'm working on it," he jauntily replied.

Across the Atlantic, Marlene Dietrich was making her own impact. Her first Hollywood movie was *Morocco* (1930). It earned her her only Academy Award nomination. She lost to the homely Marie Dressler, who took the award home for her performance in *Min and Bill*.

In *Morocco,* Dietrich made a striking appearance wearing a man's tuxedo. She shocked and titillated audiences by kissing a young lady smack on her lips. Dietrich's costume and action suggested she was bisexual, which in fact she was. She had a stream of lovers of both sexes. An equal opportunity lover! This despite a lifelong marriage to Rudolf Sieber, who had been the assistant director on her movie *The Blue Angel* and the father of the only child she would ever bear, daughter Maria. She remained devoted to them both all her life. Faithful to them in her fashion, but a source of great confusion to many, particularly the lovers she took, who found themselves as part of a strange and uncomfortable entourage.

Marlene's film career while busy was uneven, and although her fame was wide, it did not match the undiluted adulation of Coward. She was the star of a series of over-elaborate movies in which costumes, lighting, and her own mysterious sexuality detracted from the story-telling. This was not good for audiences or her career.

At one point, she was added to the list of stars that were voted "box office poison" by the Independent Theater Owners of America. She was in good company: Greta Garbo, Joan Crawford, Katharine Hepburn, and even Fred Astaire were on the same list.

She soon bounced back into popularity with her first western, *Destry Rides Again,* and in the late 1930s both she and Noël Coward had the distinction of being the top money earners in their fields.

Their careers continued to mirror one another's. The war years (1939-1945) were spent entertaining the troops. Coward singing his own compositions, including the much requested "Mad Dogs and Englishmen," to troops in the Middle East. Dietrich was on the frontlines playing to excited and horny Allied soldiers who whistled, stamped, and roared their approval.

They were always rewarded. One way or another.

After the war both Noël and Marlene suffered career spasms. Coward's high comedy style was soon replaced by John Osborne and the Angry Young Men who brought with them a new redbrick slant to the English theater. Coward's post-war musicals *Pacific 1860* and *Ace of Clubs* failed to find audiences. He was considered old-fashioned and his time was over, the pundits said.

He would eventually prove them wrong.

As for Dietrich, despite a few excellent films, notably *A Foreign Affair* (1948) and *Witness for the Prosecution* (1957), both directed by Billy Wilder, and *Judgment at Nuremberg* (1961) directed by Stanley Kramer, Marlene's post-war movies were at best forgettable.

Unable to retire—a matter of professional pride as well as finances—Dietrich embarked on a new career as a cabaret entertainer. Her appearances in Las Vegas legitimized that desert city as a venue for major stars. She persuaded her friend Noël Coward to appear there, a move that revitalized his career, as it had hers.

Having entertained the cream of café society before the outbreak of World War I, Coward now found himself embraced by the tourists who flocked to Las Vegas: "Nescafé society" he called them.

Dietrich having conquered Las Vegas, dedicated herself to concert audiences, tirelessly touring the world singing the songs she had made famous in her films, and some that she would make famous onstage.

In 1964, Coward became the first living playwright to be produced at the newly created National Theatre of Great Britain. The vehicle chosen for this occasion was dear old *Hay Fever*. Noël directed the play with an all-star cast, including Dame Edith Evans and a young "pre-Dame" Maggie Smith. "That cast could have read the Albanian Telephone Directory and held the attention of any audience."

In rehearsals Coward discovered Dame Edith had huge difficulty in remembering her lines.

"I knew them backwards last night," she moaned.

"And that is just the way you are saying them this morning," Coward retorted.

He must have thought how wonderful it was to be back at the top of his profession after ten years of semi-neglect and semi-success. He was in his element and

11

relishing every moment. He loved dealing with difficult and temperamental leading ladies. "Poor glamorous things," he would say. "All alone in the back of limousines with only huge bouquets of flowers for company."

Hay Fever was a grand success for the National Theatre, for the cast, and most importantly of all, for Coward. Thus began a period that Coward referred to as "Dad's Renaissance," and would culminate in a knighthood granted him in 1970. "Holy week," he called it.

Marlene, on the other hand, continued what she called "schlepping around the world" with her one-woman concert.

Coward made his last public appearance on the arm of Dietrich in January 1973, when they attended a performance of the revue *Oh Coward!* in New York City. It was material from his plays, other writings, and songs from his musicals cobbled together and presented by a superb cast of three. The two old friends made the difficult climb upstairs to the theater, arm in arm, holding desperately onto one another. Myrna Loy, present at the starry event, thought it was unclear who was propping up whom.

Noël came out "humming the tunes," he told waiting bystanders, but steadfastly refused all request for interviews. "I have nothing left to say." (Something I very much doubt.)

He died six weeks later, and was buried in his home in Jamaica. Perhaps he really had run out of things to say.

Dietrich continued to tour until 1975 when she staggered and fell from the stage in Sydney, Australia, breaking one of "the most beautiful legs in the world" and bringing to an end a concert career of over twenty years. She went into reclusion at her home in Paris, where she died in 1992 at the age of ninety.

With their deaths came critical re-evaluation. Writers now found their work and influence wide and lasting but still there were critics who continued to carp and label them as "shallow," "lightweight," "frivolous," and that old bugbear, the unfair "superficial."

Why not? Coward and Dietrich made everything they did appear authentic and natural. There was no sign of the hard work and endless rehearsing that went into the effect. It just looked too easy.

I believe these critics had it wrong. It wasn't Noël or Marlene who were superficial. It was the few myopic critics who couldn't see past the glamour.

The sheer longevity of their careers, Marlene's forty or so movies, her hundreds of concerts, Noël's fifty plays and more than four hundred songs, many of them now standards is a testament to the hard and constant work they brought not only to their personas, but to their crafts.

They have left a legacy that reverberates still to this day.

Hardly superficial.

CHAPTER THREE

Education

Now that I knew who my real parents were, my life became all about getting out of New Zealand and becoming a star to make my "parents" proud of me. Once this stardom was achieved, I would seek them out as equals and reveal myself as their love child.

In the meantime, I lived in a home and in a country where rugby football was followed as closely as mechanical rabbits in a greyhound race. At family dinners, my father and my brothers would re-create the most recent rugby game played in the city by moving the salt and pepper shakers, the sugar bowl, and the milk jug around the table to demonstrate the glories and failures of the game.

My life has probably been extended by this, as all my pleas to "Pass the salt, please" went unheeded and as a consequence salt never became part of my diet.

I felt totally out of place, not only in New Zealand at the bottom of the map, but in my actual home, too.

No one showed any interest or encouragement in my ambitions to become an international stage sensation. And whenever I brought it up, I was told I should have something to fall back on, in case my dreams didn't come true.

I was very unhappy at school. I was being taught by fist-faced, whisker-chinned nuns who fought me at every step. I asked them in a class called catechism what I thought were sensible questions, such as "If Adam and Eve were the first people in the world and they had two sons, Cain and Abel, how did the world continue without incest being involved?" and "If a person who ate meat on a Friday" (in Roman Catholic lore of the time, this was a mortal sin requiring an eternity in hell as punishment) "serves the same time as Hitler or Genghis Khan, how can that be considered just?"

Sister Rita, the nun to whom these questions were addressed, would slap a ruler sharply across my knuckles and tell me I lacked faith and must pray for it. She also wrote sharp and stinging letters in her slanting handwriting, which I was to take home to my parents.

After reading these blistering letters, Clive and Mary, albeit in the gentlest of manner, also accused me of lacking faith. They said they would pray for me.

I mumbled a "thank you," but I didn't see much point to it at all.

After the nuns came the Christian Brothers, a band of humorless men who were also concerned about my lack of faith.

I was bothered by Abraham being ready to kill his son (a mortal sin, surely) because God told him to, but abruptly changing his mind when God told him not to. Such lollygagging, I thought. But God was pleased and praised Abraham for his obedience, though whether for being ready to kill his son or for not killing him I was never sure. "How could his son ever trust his father again? He must have become a very muddled child in desperate need of therapy," I told Brother Whitehead, who responded by telling me I lacked faith and wrote a letter to my parents telling them to pray for me.

They said they would.

I was also bothered by the Ten Commandments. They were no help to me at all. They told me what NOT to do. "Thou shalt NOT commit adultery," "Thou shalt NOT kill," "Thou shalt NOT covet thy neighbor's wife," the latter totally irrelevant to me and not very clear

15

anyway. They did not tell one what to DO, unless you count "Honor Thy Father and Thy Mother." But what if your father was a wife-beater, a thief, a murderer? Or Abraham? You still had to honor him?

I decided that the only sin, the only crime in life, was hurting other people knowingly.

It wasn't long before I created my very own set of commandments, culled from the works of Noël Coward. They covered all contingencies, and what's more there were only four. I have tried to live my life by them, and, although I do not proselytize, I certainly pass them on to anyone who shows interest. They are:

1. Find Every Bit of Happiness Where You Can

2. Follow Your Secret Heart Your Whole Life Through

3. When Your World Is Crumbling, Sail Away! Sail Away!

4. Above All, Behave Exquisitely.

These are commandments that tell you what to DO. They can be applied to any situation that arises in life.

Now that I possessed a formula that suited me for getting through life, I stopped asking questions of the grey, dull, colorless Christian Brothers and daydreamed through dreary lessons on General Science and Chemistry (to this day I cannot tell the difference between the two). Mathematics eluded me completely, and physical education was a horror.

Instead, I busied myself finding every bit of happiness where I could.

CHAPTER FOUR

Runaway

In 1949, when I was fifteen, I decided to run away from home. I am not quite sure why. A bid for attention perhaps, or an end to unhappy, endless schooldays. I just had an urgent need to move to start my journey from the bottom of the world to the top of the world. My destination should have been London, but the travel was too costly and the problems securing a passport insurmountable for a minor such as myself, so I chose Wellington, the capital city of New Zealand, almost four hundred miles from Auckland.

I planned running away rather well, I thought.

Each day towards the end of the summer vacation, I took a suitcase of clothes and other belongings from my home to the Mount Albert railway station, where I stored the luggage in a locker. This continued for five days, until I had five suitcases in five lockers.

I had read that Dietrich traveled with seventeen pieces of matching luggage and that Coward phoned ahead for twenty-four pillows to be waiting for him in hotel rooms. I liked these extravagances, but never adopted them as my own.

Five suitcases seemed a good start.

On the day I was scheduled to return to school (Saint Peter's College, it was called) I retrieved my five suitcases from the five lockers where I had left them and clambered with difficulty aboard the train.

I did not disembark as the train drew into Mount Eden station, where a sprinkle of Saint Peter's students, looking quizzically at me, yelled, "This is our stop. Get off!"

I ignored them and looked out the train window just like Celia Johnson in the Coward film *Brief Encounter*. My mind was already on my goal. This first journey was as if I were on a provincial tour of a new play before the main event (me!) came to London and immediate success.

I remained on board until the train reached the large city terminal at the end of the local line. This is where I got off, struggling with my suitcases, and purchased a ticket to Wellington.

I also changed from my school uniform, discarding the blazer and cap, divesting myself of all connection with Saint Peter's College, and chose a brown sports coat from one of the five suitcases.

Catching sight of myself in a window, I had the look of the young Noël Coward. I just knew it. All that was missing was the cigarette in a holder. That could come later, I decided.

Whistles, the porter's cries of "all aboard," smoke billowing from the train, and I was on my way. Wellington, first stop on the provincial tour!

Marlene and Noël, Marlene and Noël, Marlene and Noël, Marlene and Noël, the wheels sang faster and faster as the train gained speed and I fell asleep.

I awoke as the train pulled into Wellington's main station.

The station porter directed me to a bed and breakfast establishment within walking distance, on a street called The Terrace. It was a slightly shabby two-story house with a "room to let" sign in the window. Noël Coward had stayed in many such establishments on his way to the top. This thought lulled me.

I gave no thought to what was happening back in Auckland. I later learned that Clive and Mary had alerted the police when I failed to return from school; they also discovered that I had not attended classes, and they heard from the boys who had left the train at the Mount Eden stop that I remained on board, surrounded by luggage.

Later I learned from my sister that she and my younger brother were very excited by my disappearance, thinking of it as something akin to a detective novel. Energized by the frenzy of activity, policeman coming and going, the phone ringing off the hook, they seemed to enjoy the hullabaloo I had caused.

My first few days in Wellington were exciting for me, too. It was the furthest I had ever traveled from Auckland; the streets and shops and trams were all foreign to me. I felt I was following in Coward's footsteps, touring in one of my own plays, fine-tuning words and scenes, ready for the wild success awaiting me in London.

As I wandered through the city, I began to think of what was ahead for me. I imagined my name in lights. I imagined clamorous ovations when I entered onstage. I thought of the flowers and telegrams crowding my dressing room. Curtain calls galore. The stamping of feet, hands red-raw from applause. I imagined bunches of admirers at the stage door.

It all seemed so real to me, so right for me. But I accomplished the journey to international fame without even beginning it. I never thought of the work that would be required to get there.

As I strolled along the streets of Wellington, I became somewhat self-pitying. Reality settling in: I had never liked reality. It was all so unfair, me being in New Zealand. There was no outlet for my "artistic" ambitions to be realized. No professional theater, no school where I could study acting. What was I to do?

I had left home without a plan. I began to feel a

fool, a failure.

I knew eventually I would have to reunite with Clive and Mary and resume dinner conversations about rugby (cricket if it was summer). But for the moment I was on my own with no idea how I could attain the stardom and acclaim I felt was mine by right of birth.

I put my doubts aside as best I could and resumed daydreaming. Back in my make-believe world, my company was sought-after. My wit entranced partygoers. I accepted invitations to New York, to the Caribbean, to Paris, to the Riviera. I would be the first New Zealander to reach such giddy heights. (This turned out to be untrue. It was Sir Edmund Hilary who became the first man to conquer Mount Everest—giddy heights indeed!)

At no point did I consider that I would have to write a play before I could tour in it. I just considered the end result. No thought was given to the process by which I would reach it.

This idiotic mind wandering came to a shattering halt a week or so after my "disappearance," when late one afternoon a uniformed man approached me and asked if I was Michael Menzies.

In the dream world where I lived, I thought to myself: "An autograph hunter, a nervous fan, an admirer bubbling with admiration."

Thrilled to be recognized, I said that I was indeed Michael Menzies. He seemed equally thrilled. He was a policeman and a promotion would be due him for finding a missing person. He asked me to accompany him to the police station.

The Wellington police called Clive and told him I was in their custody, safe and in seeming good health and spirits. (Well, why not? I had just received the most gushing and reverent notices from the *London Times* on my West End debut.)

20

The policeman told Clive that they would keep me in custody overnight until he could make arrangements for my return to Auckland.

It appeared Clive did not want me to stay in police custody and rang friends of his who lived in Wellington, asking them to collect me from the jail and allow me to stay at their house overnight. He would fly in the following morning to collect me and return me home.

His friends agreed, and in a few hours I was in the back of an Austin being driven by a man I didn't know (Clive's friend), who obviously disapproved of me, since he took me to his home in total silence.

I remember being given a meal, a sandwich I think, and a glass of milk. I sipped it as if it were champagne.

I was shown to a room with a bed that sported a feather mattress, my first and to this day the best bed I have ever slept in. I remember falling into a deep, deep sleep but not before I heard the door locked. Clive's friends were taking no chances.

When I awoke it took me quite a while to accustom myself to my surroundings. Where was I? And then I remembered: the end of the provincial tour. Clive would be arriving shortly. I steeled myself for his anger.

Shortly I heard his voice thanking my "hosts." Then I heard the sound of a key unlocking the door.

I was sitting on the high bed, fully dressed and kicking my legs to and fro.

Clive had tears in his eyes and was smiling like a river.

"It's so good to see you, son," he said, beaming.

I was surprised out of my skin. I was expecting a barrage of "how-dare-you-do-this-to-your-mother" and "don't-you-realize-how-worried-we-were?" Certainly not "It's so good to see you, son." I was very much taken aback.

He hugged and kissed me, and with each display of

affection on his part my guilt grew. I withdrew into myself. I didn't know how to explain myself and my crazed actions.

At that moment I joined the ranks of the most highly bemused persons of all time: an adolescent without the questions and certainly without the answers.

Soon we were on a plane, my first ever flight, looking down on patchwork farms, tiny and tidy viewed from the air, lakes like puddles, mountains topped with snow. (I had never seen snow before.)

It was a magic flight, but I daren't show pleasure, for I had done something terribly bad by running away from home. And I couldn't answer the question "Why had I done so?" which I knew would be asked and demanded by Clive and Mary.

I felt a rush of shame. They had never shown cruelty to me, and there was no reason for me to run away from their care, an action that had kept them awake with worry, going over and over again what they had done to cause this (nothing really) as they faced the nightmare of possibilities that could have happened to me.

All I said—and it was the truth—was, "I don't know why."

I did give my word that I would never do anything as stupid and careless and as unkind as that again, and I never did. Soon I was back in my own bed.

But the agony of adolescence would remain with me for a few more years.

With reluctance, but swayed by Clive's pleading, the Christian Brothers accepted me back into Saint Peter's, where my notoriety gave me a few weeks of tepid popularity from my fellow pupils. The interest and popularity faded very quickly, however. Then it was back to my daydreaming.

CHAPTER FIVE

Kumeu

Everything connected with either Coward or Dietrich, I researched, listened to, read, or endlessly mulled over in my mind. Their music became the soundtrack of my days: Coward singing his own songs with a caressing voice, almost a light soprano at times. When it came to his patter songs, such as "Mad Dogs and Englishmen" and "Don't Put Your Daughter on the Stage, Mrs. Worthington," he displayed a verve and syncopation totally his own.

He had written once that the only people in the world with perfect pitch were Lily Pons and himelf. For years I wasn't sure if this was said jokingly or seriously.

Dietrich's husky, dark voice with a surprisingly small range enchanted me. She was champagne, late nights, cigarette smoke, Molyneux gowns, limousines, bouquets of flowers, perfume, amber lighting, everything I felt was mine by birthright and certainly mine by desire. (Well, perhaps not the Molyneux gowns.)

I read that Coward wrote *Hay Fever* in three days, *Private Lives* in four, and *Blithe Spirit* in six. It never occurred to me to consider the gestation period: the thought and care and re-working of plot and character that could last over a year before he put pen to paper. The nights he slept worrying over a plot point, the days he walked and walked, going over dialogue and character development– none of this occurred to me at all.

With his light-hearted, breezy writing and staccato dialogue, he made everything seem easy.

So I, too, would write a play, produce it, and star in it. I would prove to the world that I was his son and that he had passed his talent on to me, even if it was unwittingly. I would be on my way!

It would take me no longer than a week to write the play. Word of its dazzling success would somehow reach London, and I would be whisked there and become a star in no time flat.

I would invite Coward and Dietrich to the opening night. At the party afterwards (Claridge's? The Savoy? The Ivy?) the reviews, one more splendid than the next, would keep arriving and being read aloud to the crowd that had gathered there (Claridge's? The Savoy? The Ivy?). I would then take Coward and Dietrich aside and tell them they were my parents, I was their son.

What a night that would be!

With startling naiveté and the help of a friend pleasingly named David Desmond Grant, I hired a bare church hall with hard church pew benches in a rural community about twenty-five miles from my home, in a place called Kumeu. This was 1951 and I was now almost seventeen years old.

I enlisted six friends as supporting actors, but never gave them scripts, for I never bothered to commit the play to paper. I just told them the story I had created (lost now in a fog of memory). Coward wrote his plays in less than a week, staged them, and voila, success! I could do that.

I cannot recall the plot of my play (if in fact there was one) because so deep is my embarrassment and so completely have I erased this impulsive and mad adolescent act from my memory that it cannot be recalled.

I even shudder to write the title I gave my play:

Fifi Says "Oui!" I thought it sounded extremely sophisticated and bristling with a risqué quality that would ensure all 452 residents of Kumeu would rush to attend the church hall production.

Such pride. So dazzlingly out of touch. Such a lazy and cavalier attitude, another facet of my personality that has lasted throughout my lifetime. Not inherited from Noël or Marlene, nor for that matter from Clive and Mary.

Ten people (two of them Clive and Mary) attended the performance. (ONE NIGHT ONLY! screamed a cardboard poster with crooked lettering picked out in silver glitter.) Two of the audience (not Clive and Mary) noisily left fifteen minutes into my pitiful performance.

None of the six friends whom I had chosen as my supporting cast had any clue when to enter onstage or what to say when they did. At least I think I had told them when to come in and what to say. They had never been rehearsed when all was said and done. I felt they would know what I wanted them to do by sheer osmosis.

Would they remember?

They waited in the wings with the air of persons about to mount the executioner's block. Garbed in silk dressing gowns and sporting cigarettes uneasily lodged in long ivory holders, my idea of Coward characters, they stood there, dimly shaking, dreading the whole evening, no doubt hoping the ground would open up and they would disappear.

I felt the audience sinking deeper into their hard, uncomfortable seats and whispering conspiratorially to one another. To stimulate their interest, I would wave one of my trembling actor/friends onto the stage to join me in my pathetic babbling.

At my urging they shuffled onstage and stood there, guiltily, speechless, at a total loss.

Desperately trying to regain the attention of the audience already on the brink of mutiny, I began a rambling monologue about my imagined parentage, interrupted by a loud and puzzled query from a red-faced man sitting alone in the fourth row center: "Who's this Noël Coward and Marlene what's-her-name?" I babbled on about what a sensation I was going to cause when (I didn't even consider *if*) I arrived in London. "Both Broadway and Hollywood had better watch out!" I cried out in a warning that was never heeded.

Instead it was poor, innocent Kumeu that had to watch out. Witness to the inane exhibitionism of a teenager who just wanted out of New Zealand.

After about ten minutes of my brazen self-advertising, which felt like a dozen years, the audience was becoming restless and hostile, as were the six actor/friends now sharing the stage with me in bewildered embarrassment. I motioned for the curtain to be drawn. The applause was non-existent. The audience exited hurriedly in case there was any more of this shameful nonsense to come.

As far as my six actor/friends were concerned, I never saw nor spoke to them again. Their anger, humiliation, and embarrassment coupled with my own, created valid reasons for this split. The end of teenage friendships. We would cross the street if we saw each other coming our way. We remained silent if we met in the same restaurant. Cold stares.

David Desmond Grant and I went for a desultory swim in Mission Bay a couple of days later but didn't have much to say to one another. (He looked heart-stoppingly, mouth-wateringly good in a green Speedo, and he is the only thing about this whole experience I recall with any kind of pleasure.) But even he and I soon bleakly lost touch with one another.

It was no comfort for me to recall Coward was roundly booed on the opening night of one his plays, *Sirocco*, and spat at when he left the stage door. At least he had spent time writing and rehearsing it. He was anything but lazy and ill-prepared.

On the drive home, Clive said to me, "Your play seemed rather short" (it had clocked in at thirty three minutes). Mary added a sigh-like, "Yes, it was." I got the impression that they both wished it had been even shorter.

As with my running away to Wellington, we never referred to it again.

CHAPTER SIX

Bedside Talks

It was around this time that Mary took to her bed.

I like to think I had nothing to do with this, but since her "illnesses" were never diagnosed, remaining vague and something to do with her "insides," I cannot be sure of this. Dr. MacCormack came every week with his stethoscope around his neck and carrying a Gladstone bag. He examined Mary, prescribed pills, and said he didn't quite know what was wrong, but bed rest couldn't hurt. Mary's sister Lillian believed it was all play-acting.

So Mary stayed in bed, wearing what was then called a "matinee jacket," reading thrillers and eating Heard's Hard Toffee. Clive took over running the household with the help of a series of housekeepers all named after flowers: Daphne, Lily, Pansy, and Lilac. The very last one ("a Communist" my mother sniffed) was named Mercy, thus ending the floral invasion of our home. Of all of them I liked Mercy best. It was probably her name; it had a reassuring ring to it.

Each of us children was allowed ten minutes solo time with Mary after dinner, so as not to "overtire" her. My time with my mother was spent chattering about Marlene's films and how beautiful she was. "She has hooded eyes, like a cobra's," I would gush. I would tell my mother the story of Dietrich's films. Generally, Marlene was either a spy or suspected of being one, often a cabaret singer thrown into the bargain, and her movies ended when either she died or gave up the love of her life.

Once memorably in *Morocco*, she removed her high-heeled shoes and, barefoot, followed Gary Cooper, who had joined the Foreign Legion, into the desert. Marlene was wearing nothing but a chiffon dress. No handbag, no hat.

"No handbag? No hat in the desert?" Mary spoke disbelievingly.

"She had a scarf," I said defensively.

"Sounds just like real life," Mary murmured.

She had had enough of this Marlene talk.

Mary sighed and told me her greatest regret was in marrying too young and having a family soon after, which prevented her indulging in her greatest wish, which was to travel the world over. This translated to my mind as "don't get married and make sure I travel," advice I gladly took and resolutely followed.

Much later I learned from my sister that her evening talks with our mother resulted in her being told that the best thing Mary ever did was marrying young and having children soon after. My sister followed this advice.

I think Mary instinctively knew what each of her children wanted and gently guided us along those paths in our bedroom chats after dinner.

One of my brothers has no recollection of their talks, other than Mary begging him to stop kicking the side of her bed while they spoke. This, I know, blows right out of the water my theory of Mary knowing what was best for her children, although who knows? My brother may well be better off for not kicking beds.

The major result of my Kumeu horror was that I decided not to write any more plays…well, at least not in the immediate future.

But Noël Coward was also an actor. Perhaps that was where my future lay. I could impress him with my acting skills and thus be accepted by him as his long lost son.

At the time, New Zealand had no professional theater (that was to come later). But amateur companies flourished and productions were mounted willy-nilly with more ambition than accomplishment. In giddy succession, I appeared in plays where I bewildered audiences with my range. I was a preacher, a Chinaman, a Gestapo, a hussar, a scorned lover, and most strange of all, an ant!

This seemed to me sufficient stage experience to travel half a world away, live my mother's dream for herself ("travel and don't marry"), as well as my own ("travel and don't marry"), and make my London stage debut. I had saved a little money and was now prepared to see the world.

Oddly and only I fear in retrospect did I realize it was with great understanding and extraordinary generosity that Clive and Mary said they would match my savings pound for pound. I'd earned a modest amount writing copy at an advertising agency. ("Roma, the dust-freed tea" comes to mind.) These monies would go to my goal of reaching London, gaining international respect and success, and the long-awaited and highly charged emotional meeting with Noël and Marlene.

Clive and Mary could see I was determined to leave New Zealand, and they would put nothing in my way.

Mary urged me to live a good life, so that we could meet again in heaven.

"That's somewhere in Wyoming, isn't it?" I impertinently replied.

CHAPTER SEVEN
Peace in Our Time

While saving money to leave New Zealand, I appeared with almost all the amateur theater groups in Auckland. It would stand me in good stead, I reasoned, when I arrived in London, ready to be cast in West End productions.

The lack of male actors was the reason for my many stage appearances. This was a direct result of the New Zealand attitude towards art in those days, particularly the males who embraced it. Theater was "sissy stuff" at best; downright "fag" behavior at worst. Men played rugby, soccer, and cricket, drank beer, and were the only parent working. None of this single mom nonsense.

Friends of Clive and Mary would ask after me. "Does he still act?" they'd inquire in the manner they might say, "Does he still knit?"

But before I left for England and my inevitable reunion with Noël and Marlene, I wanted to appear in a Coward play in Auckland.

I was nineteen, bony, pimply, pseudo-sophisticated, and full of myself.

One of the amateur theater groups announced they were auditioning actors for a play by Coward called *Peace in Our Time.* It sported a big cast, and I was confident that I would be selected for one role or another. It didn't matter to me the size of the part: what was important was that I appear in a Coward play, so when I met The Master, I could discuss it knowledgably

31

and he would be very impressed.

Peace in Our Time poses the fascinating question: how would Britain have reacted if the Germans had won the Battle of Britain and occupied the country? The play takes place in a London pub, the Shy Gazelle, where a resistance group is formed despite the presence of Nazi officers and British quislings sharing the pub with them.

I was cast as Kurt Forster, who did not make an appearance until the third act. My entrance was on the arm of one of the British quislings, the editor of a newspaper very conciliatory to the German occupiers. He was, in fact, a collaborator, and although not spelled out, there was the suggestion that we (that is, the editor and me) were lovers.

After reading it, Mary told me she disapproved of the play and was not well enough to attend. Clive said, "Good for you, son," but also declined to come.

My character made sure that the people in the play knew he was Austrian rather than German. He was a production designer at Covent Garden Opera and talked patronizingly of the superiority of German opera to a group of disinterested Britishers who were drinking watered down beer, the only alcohol available to them.

The audience appeared equally disinterested.

During the course of my scene, my character would click his heels together, raise his glass on high, and toast "Heil, Hitler!" which did not go down well. A drink is "accidentally" spilled on Kurt and he storms out.

That was the extent of my scene. I enjoyed the storming out bit quite a lot.

I couldn't wait to tell Coward about my experiences in his play, and the hidden meanings I had found in the script, all with unerring inaccuracy.

Since my entrance was late into the piece, I had the men's dressing room at the Saint Andrew's Church hall to myself after Act II had begun. I experimented with makeup in the belief I was making myself effeminate, when in fact no makeup at all would have given the same result. I *was* effeminate.

My costume featured equestrian-style boots (not quite sure why, since no horse was ever mentioned) and a form-fitting tunic with the trousers tucked into the boots. Much mirror checking, many "Heil, Hitlers!" but still it wasn't right. Something was missing.

Of course! Kurt Forster would have blond hair.

Clive had made me a handsome makeup case, heavy as could be, with a lock and a key and trays that folded out and places for various Leichner fives and nines and Crimson Lakes, cold cream, and powder puffs. Among the goodies in this box was a container of gold dust. I applied a little to the sides of my hair. Perfect!

Buoyed by my reflection in the mirror, I applied a liberal amount of gold dust all over my scalp, hiding my brown tresses until I was glowing like a sun god. Still perfect!

The time came for my entrance. I left the dressing room and made my way to the wings, where I met up with the actor who played the quisling editor and my paramour, and locked arms with him.

We made a brazen entrance, and when it came time for me to click my heels and cry "Heil, Hitler!" I did so with supreme confidence and authority.

The audience fell out of their seats with laughter.

This response both puzzled and worried me. *Why were they laughing?* I thought to myself. *This is a serious play and my scene is very dramatic.*

It wasn't until I left the stage that I found the reason for the laughter. My grand gesture of toasting and the click of my heels dislodged the gold dust in my hair, causing it to flutter into a heap of gold dust on the floor.

Michael Menzies

Perhaps I would not discuss this appearance in one of Coward's plays with The Master after all.

CHAPTER EIGHT

London at Last!

When finally I had enough money, I purchased a one-way ticket to London on a ship named *Johann van Oldenbarnevelt*. I had neither arranged a job nor lodging for my arrival. I simply assumed in my normal foolhardy manner that there would be no problem.

The *Johann van Oldenbarnevelt* had been built by the Dutch for their Far East Indian trade in the early part of the twentieth century. It was then converted to a troop ship in World War II, chugging soldiers here and there. After the war it became a one class P&O liner wearily sailing the seas, falling exhausted into port after port, gathering itself together after unloading bananas (it always seemed to be bananas), and then staggering onto the next port of call, where it unloaded more bananas and replaced them with even more bananas, presumably fresher ones.

The *Johann van Oldenbarnevelt* later changed its name to *Lakonia* and shortly afterwards sank like a boulder in the Bay of Biscay, where it remains to this day, its cargo of bananas hardly worth the effort of finding the ship and bringing it to the surface.

After seven weeks at sea and eight ports of call, the *Johann van Oldenbarnevelt* eventually reached Southampton, where all the passengers were disembarked and taken by train to London. It was May 5, 1956 and I had turned twenty years old.

Before I could put into operation the things I was sure would lead to the shining stage career that lay ahead for me, I had to find a place to live. (A small bed-sitting room in Muswell Hill, with a gas ring and fire, both fed by shillings would do for the moment.)

I also had to learn the Underground System—"the tube" it was called—and how to get into the West End where the theaters were, and of course, I had to buy a ticket to a show.

There was no question which play I would choose for my first experience. At the Lyric Theatre on Shaftesbury Avenue, H.M. Tennant, the most prestigious and opulent of London producers, was presenting Vivien Leigh in *South Sea Bubble,* a new comedy by Noël Coward! It is a slight play, one of The Master's lesser works, and because of what would be seen today as frightening political incorrectness, totally unrevivable.

But on that spring evening in London, I was enchanted, transported, bewitched, enthralled. My heart was beating so hard it could barely stay in my chest. With no critical eye, no comparisons, no real knowledge of theater, I was in another world: one of beauty and wit. A world I desperately wanted to live in.

The pace of the play was speedway-fast: characters overlapping dialogue, words spilling out, a feeling of urgency but in spite of its speed, every word clearly understood. The play was always human, and best of all, always witty. The setting was sumptuous—Act I: a verandah on a tropical island in blazing sunlight overlooking a glistening sea, Act II: a verandah on a tropical island shimmering in full moonlight, and finally in Act III, back to the verandah on the tropical island in blazing sunlight, still overlooking a glistening sea.

And Vivien Leigh! In person! In front of me, onstage! Scarlett O'Hara. Lady Hamilton. Blanche du Bois. Her entrance was a star's entrance: much talk of her character before she appeared so that one was full of anticipation waiting for her arrival. When at last she made her entrance, she ran lightly onto the stage, feet hardly touching the ground, sort of floating, to greet a great friend (a part I was sure I could have played). Delighted to see him she gushed words of welcome and apology for her lateness. With a smile that lit up the entire theater, she welcomed him onto the verandah on a tropical island in blazing sunlight overlooking a glistening sea. Leigh was the splendor of the play—fragile, delicate, and porcelain-like. Her beauty timeless, and as one critic wrote, "Her performance shines like the stars, and is as troubling as the inconstant moon."

It was an amazing revelation to me. I had never been privy to such professionalism on every level. Acting, set design, lighting, costumes, all were of a standard way beyond my experience and way beyond my imagination. I could hardly contain my emotions during the first act interval, so anxious was I to return to the magic of the play.

However, a niggling self-doubt snuck into my consciousness. Was I sufficiently prepared to be an actor? Could I compete, could I keep up with performers like this? I was witnessing a quality, a level I knew I could never reach.

I dismissed the thought as quickly as it had entered my head. This was not a night for such questions. This was a night to let words, beauty, and Coward's wit sweep over me like a wave. Tomorrow I could view the results, analyze the situation, change direction if need be. For now, I would let nothing break the spell.

I returned to my seat when the warning bell sounded. The house lights dimmed, sending shivers up my spine, the curtain rose and once again I was in another world: totally absorbed by what was happening on the verandah on that tropical island.

The two hours of the play flew by like two

minutes, and on leaving the theater, I ran, I skipped, I jumped, I laughed, I wept, I shouted, I sang. I was three feet off the ground. I have no recollection of how I found my way back to Muswell Hill and my tiny bed-sitting room. It had to have been by the tube. Or perhaps it was a trip on gossamer wings!

I was too excited to sleep. Vivien Leigh was dancing through my mind. I had achieved part of my dream. I was in London. The center of things. The top of the map.

Ah, but the other part of my dream: becoming an actor, appearing on the West End stage and achieving major success, became less and less certain. Thoughts that kept tumbling around in my head that night, ever-changing, troubling, made me uneasy. The idea of me becoming a star began to retreat from my consciousness, slowly at first, and then, like a film speeded up, racing away in a fast blur. Soon that dream would totally disappear.

The initial excitement of the evening was replaced by exhaustion, by doubt, and then, thankfully, sleep finally overcame me.

I awoke in Muswell Hill, with a realization as forceful as thunder: the theater was not where I was meant to be. I had no place in it, certainly not as a writer/actor/composer. I would never be another Noël Coward. I suppose I had my doubts all along, but seeing Vivien Leigh in that performance snapped me wide awake to the absurdity of my dream.

It gradually occurred to me that I was born to appreciate. I was born to be a member of the audience. I had a talent to recognize and celebrate others' talent. But none of my own. Curiously, the emotion that flooded through me when this realization dawned on me was not regret but one of immense relief. I didn't have to do all the hard work to become famous. I didn't have to focus my energies on a single goal. I didn't have to study. I had always wanted my life to be easy.

Although Coward gave the impression of making everything he did seem easy, without effort, I knew that this was not so. I came to learn that his accomplishments were hard earned and hard won.

As for me, I was born lazy—all that New Zealand sunshine, I assume, was to blame. Not only was I lazy, I had to admit to certain foolishness as well: I had no Plan B. I had relied entirely on my daydreaming for my future, and it had now burst, like last night's *Bubble*. It was a jolt to find I was left without direction or ambition, dangerously and worryingly ill-prepared for life.

My obsession with Coward and Dietrich had not prepared me for anything. As Clive and Mary had pointed out regularly, I had nothing to fall back on. It flew in the face of everything one had been told. Get ahead, work hard. But what about enjoy life?

I wasn't interested in getting ahead (how could I anyway? I was appallingly ill-educated, fit for nothing, really) Working hard? (Anathema to me.) What to do now? I concentrated on the last option: enjoy life.

I stayed in bed the entire next day considering my limited choices. A day in bed like Mary, but without the thrillers and Heard's Hard Toffee. I could blame no one else but myself for this dilemma. I had made my own bed, and now I had to lie on it.

I got out of bed.

I donned a dressing gown and went down the hall to a communal bathroom, inserted a shilling in a hot water heater called a califont, and took a long hot bath.

While luxuriating in the bathtub, I had a sort of epiphany. I decided that instead of trying to arrange destiny to meet my desires, I would simply allow life to sweep over me, take me where it would, to mountaintops or deep hidden valleys. I would not resist nor would I try to manipulate it. Rather, I would simply follow it.

I would follow my own secret heart. After all, that was one of my four commandments.

I felt much better. I did not have to work to become famous after all. A weight off my shoulders, a mind suddenly and mysteriously at rest.

Finally I had something to fall back on: life—fate, destiny, call it what you will.

I got out of the bath, dried myself, returned to my room, and got back in bed.

What was I capable of? It didn't really matter. I was in London, thousands of miles away from New Zealand. My eyes closed, and in that half world between consciousness and sleep, I heard Scarlett O'Hara whispering in my ear, "I'll think about that tomorrow."

And in seconds I was blissfully asleep, a smile on my face.

After all, tomorrow is another day.

CHAPTER NINE

Dietrich in Performance

By this time, the belief that Coward and Dietrich were my real parents had vanished—poof!—like a magic act, the rabbit no longer in the hat. But after so many years of devotion to and love for them, I continued to hold them in the highest esteem and thought of them still as having a kind of cosmic connection to me.

I now wanted to meet them, if only to tell them how grateful I was for the manner in which they inspired me. If it weren't for them, I would still be in New Zealand looking for "something to fall back on." But because of them I was in a much better place. I was in London looking for something to fall back on.

I was still uncertain what London offered me, but I knew with absolute certainty that it had more options for me than New Zealand. I could sell programs in a theater, I could become a receptionist at a grand hotel, I could work in Liberty's store measuring out luxury fabric by the yard. It wasn't an impossible dream that in one of these jobs I would meet either Coward or Dietrich.

Despite my adoration of her, Dietrich did not occupy as large a role in my thoughts as Coward did. Most of my knowledge of her was gleaned from seeing her on the cinema screen and reading about her in movie magazines.

Obviously her world-weary persona appealed to me. I was enamored of her unique and sullen beauty. The cathedral arch of her penciled eyebrows, the lush sensuality of her lips, the slouch that emphasized her hips and made clothes look as though they were draped on her—all of this I loved and admired.

And those legs!—the swell of thigh, the curve of calf, the sheer breath-taking elegance of ankle. I wanted nothing more than to fall asleep to her singing me a soft lullaby, a cloud of perfume following her as she left my room on her way to a party that began when she arrived and ended the moment she left.

As I wandered around London's West End, familiarizing myself with the theaters and restaurants and clubs that I wanted to be part of, I passed the famous Café de Paris nightclub.

It was here Marlene Dietrich made her first cabaret appearance in London in June 1954, two years prior to my arrival. If only I had been present.

The month long season was sold out before she even arrived in England. The press (this was pre-television) heralded her appearance with as much fervor as a coronation – and a sort of coronation it was. Her film career in jeopardy, she nonetheless remained a Movie Star. Countless interviews were conducted from the lush comfort of the lushly designed Oliver Messel suite at the Dorchester Hotel where she stayed.

I had read and re-read everything I could find about her opening night until I convinced myself I had been there. I knew from the reportage that the Café de Paris was decorated in red velvet and gold leaf frou frou, featured over-the-top chi chi chandeliers, and had a horseshoe staircase that led to a small stage area. It was a perfect setting for a cabaret sensation such as Marlene.

I longed to go inside to see where she had performed, to touch the staircase railing her fingers had strayed down, but it was outrageously expensive and I could not afford entry. Frequently I would stand outside the nightclub with a pleading, lingering look on my face, hoping the bouncer would lift the velvet rope and beckon me in to see the current headliner. He never did.

From avid perusal of magazines of the time, I learned the opening night audience for Dietrich's engagement arrived three hours before the midnight concert was to occur, and that they exceeded the fire regulations governing occupancy by nearly a third. No one was asked to leave, no one complained. Who would?

Extra mounted police were assigned to the area to control the crowds who came to see the celebrity audience arrive in glittering finery.

Each night of her run, she was introduced by a different male star of sufficient magnitude to be considered her equal, or at least a near equal. The first was to be her great friend Noël Coward. He would be followed by Laurence Olivier, Michael Redgrave, Robert Morley, Alec Guinness, and many more, a parade of famous men.

Her opening night included royalty, famous people, rich people, society people, business executives, every stage and film star who wasn't otherwise engaged, and even some who were. Those who were performing themselves rushed to the Café de Paris from their own theaters still in their stage makeup in order to be in attendance.

Excitement mounted as midnight approached and Noël Coward appeared. Applause greeted him. People leaned forward in anticipation. Coward stood at the base of the sweeping staircase to introduce her. In his clipped voice, rolling his "Rs," he recited a poem he had written especially for the occasion. It had been designed to arouse the audience to fever pitch. And it did!

He proclaimed the last word of his poem with a flourish. It was her name: "Marlene!" He stretched all three syllables as if it were taffy—raising his hand in an airy salute—and there, stepping into her spotlight at the top of the stairs appeared The Queen of the World: Marlene Dietrich!

She stood unflinchingly still as wild applause enveloped her. Slowly, eyes ahead, never looking down, a trick she learned from Las Vegas showgirls, she began a regal descent of the stairs as the orchestra started a measured vamp, which must have built an electric thrill in her worshipful audience. Halfway down she paused, shrugging her swans down coat off her alabaster shoulders to reveal the famous "nude" dress—a major piece of complicated engineering by Jean Louis, himself a Hollywood legend.

The nude dress was to become a staple of all future Dietrich performances. It was made from flesh colored soufflé chiffon fabric, and hugging the curves of her frame, gave the illusion that she was naked. The addition of strategically placed pearls, mirrors, diamonds, and rhinestones scattered across her breasts, and cleverly arranged at her throat suggesting a necklace, which was in fact part of the garment. The gown was transparent enough to give the impression you could see everything and opaque enough to realize you were seeing nothing.

She surveyed her audience from her snake-hooded eyes, a slight smile playing around her lips. And then, with a small kick that cleverly re-arranged her coat (this one gesture rehearsed for hours until it attained perfection), she gained the small stage and whispered sexily into the microphone, "Hello."

The audience roared their welcome.

What followed was sheer magic. A concert of forty minutes, concluding when she announced, "This is the last one, and the inevitable one." The audience went wild as they recognized the first few notes of her signature song, "Falling in Love Again."

When encores were insistently demanded she

ignored them, taking her last bows and gently scolding the audience, "I told you that was the last one."

Everything was superb, each song first-rate, a never-before experience; she became the toast of the town, the hottest, most difficult ticket to secure. Back at the top of her profession, not the best of singers, not the best of dancers, but possessing an indefinable magic, she had total, unmistakable star quality. One cannot describe star quality, but like pornography, one knows it when one sees it.

Reviews were ecstatic: *Variety* enthused "Exceptional," while the *Evening News* headlined its review with "Sheer Rapture." Superlatives tripping over superlatives.

Of course, I got all of this second hand. I had read about in New Zealand, savored and remembered as much as I could. It was an Occasion, an Event, and to this day, I regret I could not be there to witness it and take part in all of the hoopla. I was two years too late. Every time I passed the Café de Paris, I thought of Marlene and her opening night.

For years she traveled the world—theaters, hotel ballrooms, cabarets—hypnotizing audiences, leaving them mesmerized, full of wonder and awe. She was an illusion, a creation of smoke and mirrors, of imagination and lighting. No one who saw her could ever forget her.

Kenneth Tynan, the brilliant and often-barbed critic, had written of her, "She has sex without gender"—probably the best explanation of Marlene Dietrich's unique and extraordinary appeal. In men's wear she appealed to women. In her nude dress she rendered strong men pale.

Eventually, I would get to see her in concert on five different occasions: twice in London and three times in New York. No other artist has made my heart beat faster or my pulse race more. I was never disappointed, never wanted her concerts to end, and I was enslaved anew each time by her beauty, her glamour, her magic, and the voice that broke my heart every time I heard her sing.

Dietrich's curtain calls were a show of their own, each different and most nights never less than twenty. All were staged: the first caught her walking upstage, her coat trailing behind her, a hand on her heart and a look over her shoulder that said "This much applause? For me?" A teasing smile and an exchange between star and audience that indicated "Well, I deserve it, don't I?" The second curtain—a peek-a-boo look through drawn drapes—"Are you still there?" she seemed to say. Handsome, handpicked young men in tuxedos would run down the aisles of the venues she appeared in throwing roses at her until it seemed she was knee-deep in flowers. More and more curtain calls followed. Climax after climax until everyone was spent.

Then the final moment—a deep, deep bow—the swift, last fall of the curtain and the theater lights came up. Despite the continuing cheers and applause, despite the floor-stamping demands from the audience, the show was over.

Dietrich always left them wanting more.

Eventually the excitedly chattering, thoroughly satisfied audience left the theater. Many of them unable to accept that the evening was over crowded the stage door. Another show took place as Marlene exited, extravagant flowers in the crook of one arm, the other used for passing out signed photographs. She was superbly coiffed, made up and elegantly suited (Chanel? Dior?). One was tempted to kiss the hem of her garment.

I was present one night outside the Mark Hellinger Theatre in New York when, with the help of two young men, she climbed onto the hood of her Rolls Royce and posed, her legs exquisitely displayed, her appreciation of our devotion to her almost equal to our adulation. From the hood of the car, her eyes met mine and we exchanged smiles. In that moment I knew she knew I was hers.

CHAPTER TEN
Filing Clerk

Once I realized that my dreams of fame were never to occur, my first decision was to move from my bed-sitting room in Muswell Hill (then a very suburban area) to a basement flat in Draycott Place off Sloane Square, a much more fashionable address, only blocks away from Coward's London home.

As glad as I was to be there, I knew no one in London. I began to feel a little lonely, homesick even, and what's more I was running out of the meager savings I had left. I had to find a job.

My lack of education was a tremendous handicap. My formal learning had come to a shuddering halt when I turned fifteen. This was the legal age at which New Zealand boys and girls could go out into the world. The Christian Brothers were very happy to see me go, and I was very happy to leave them.

I had not learned anything useful from my New Zealand schooling. However, I did know the alphabet, at last something to fall back on. Through an employment agency advertising summer jobs for "temporary workers," I secured a post as a filing clerk at a firm called J. L. Morison & Son in Albemarle Street. I cannot recall what they did. Insurance? Exporting? Importing? No matter.

At lunch one day in the office break room, I told my colleagues an incident that occurred on my trip from Auckland to London.

The story started when the *Johann van*

Oldenbarnevelt had navigated the length of the Suez Canal. While the ship was loading or unloading bananas at Port Said, I joined many of my fellow passengers on a day trip ashore to Cairo to visit the Pyramids and the Sphinx. The story I told at lunch that day occurred on that side trip to Cairo, and involved the death of a camel.

My co-workers put aside their paper bag lunches with boiled eggs and ham sandwiches slightly curling at the edges and listened to me with rapt attention, a reaction I was totally unused to and rather liked. There was much laughter as I told the story and I began to feel welcome among them. I belonged in London. I needn't be lonely. There were friends to be made. It was a good feeling.

As I was relating my story, I realized they no longer regarded me as a "temp" but as one of them, a fellow colleague. They besieged me with requests for more stories of my travels. I was even invited to a party to re-tell my camel story.

A Miss Pinkerton, who ran the filing department and looked as though she had been knitted and was slowly unraveling, took me aside afterwards and said she felt I was wasted filing in the A to Z department. She said I should write down the tale I had told at the lunch table, for she had found it particularly interesting, and try to have it published.

No matter that my last attempt at writing, *Fifi Says "Oui!"*, had been dismal, it was a very tempting suggestion.

I used Miss Pinkerton's Olivetti typewriter (after hours and with her permission) and sent the story, which I had coyly entitled "I Kill Camels With Blue Grass," to *Vogue* magazine because they had featured Marlene Dietrich on a recent cover. Had she been on the cover of *Popular Mechanics,* I guess I would have sent it there. I never expected to hear from *Vogue.* I considered writing a career in which I had already failed.

I was staggered therefore when four weeks later, *Vogue* sent me a check for three guineas and said they planned to publish my story in the August issue, which thrilled me no end. It thrilled Miss Pinkerton no end, too.

Who knew that getting published was so easy? This accomplishment gave me the gumption to leave J.L. Morison & Son and try my hand as a writer. I even had "writer" printed in my passport under "occupation." Sadly, it looked more like "waiter" than "writer."

Were the fates trying to send me a signal?

And if so, was it to pursue writing? Or become a waiter?

CHAPTER ELEVEN

"I Kill Camels With Blue Grass"

This is the camel story that *Vogue* published in the August issue. I was now twenty-two and eager to begin the next part of my life.

When I was told I would have to go by camel to see the pyramids, I was outraged.

"It was my belief," I imperiously noted, "that one traveled by Cadillac in the desert."

"It is great fun on a camel," the Egyptian travel agent said.

"Gracious," I replied with disbelief, "I have never been in a Cadillac." I became wistful. "I have been in a Lincoln Continental," I added somewhat irrelevantly.

"Everybody goes to the pyramids on a camel."

That was just sales talk, I decided. I was sure Sheikh Rashould Al Thing or whatever his name was never set a slippered foot near a camel. I had read an article all about him in *Life* magazine, together with some quite alarming photographs. He was peering from the back seat of a powder blue Cadillac (they were colored photographs) parked alongside an oasis, and once it seemed, alongside a mirage.

"Have you ever been on a camel, sir?"

"No, never."

"You will enjoy. Soft swaying motion. Very nice."

"Is it anything like a Ferris wheel?" I became anxious.

"Nothing like a Ferris wheel." The travel agent was becoming testy. He smiled as though his mouth was full of vinegar

Several of the people in the line behind me, dying to see the pyramids and evidently mad to go by camel, were becoming restive.

"Do you," exclaimed an irate lady whose left breast proclaimed she was Betty Lou and came from Memphis, Tennessee, "or do you not want to go to see the pyramids?"

"My dearest wish," I murmured. "By Cadillac," I added.

Betty Lou breathed heavily, which caused a sort of earthquake in the Memphis area.

"There are only camels," she boomed at me. "The wog keeps telling you that. Pardon me," she said to the wog. "My nerves," she exclaimed. "I was in Tehran yesterday."

I wondered why she was in Tehran yesterday and if that city was bad for nerves, and then I wondered why my mind wandered so, and I booked for a camel trip to see the pyramids, all in one breath.

My camel, the suspicious looking guide told me, was gentle, and its name was Zasu Pitts. "My camels— they are all named after the film stars, no?" he gloated.

I couldn't help thinking that my camel was probably the oldest camel in the desert, and it wasn't very reassuring to find Betty Lou on a camel named Marlon Brando.

"Gee," she announced rather loudly, "my cousin Myrtle will be tickled pink to learn I've been to see the lil ol' Sphinx on Marlon Brando." Her Memphis badge went up and down with delight.

Marlon Brando did not.

"Imagine!" I said, wondering who would be tickled pink to hear that I went on Zasu Pitts. The only one I could think of who would be was Zasu Pitts, and I didn't know her and had no way of letting her know. (I don't think she was under a studio contract so a letter addressed to her at RKO or Warner Brothers was out of the question.)

The suspicious guide, a shiny brown gentleman with shifty eyes and sweaty brow, motioned me towards my animal, which obligingly sank, swaying more dangerously than softly, I thought.

I clambered on to Miss Pitts who arose to the order of the shiny brown gentleman. "Very comfortable, no?" he hissed at me.

"Yes. I mean no. I have keys in my back pocket, you see."

"Very comfortable," he insisted in a most sinister manner, so I smiled wanly, attempting to be agreeable.

After all, I didn't want to cause a scene in the desert.

"Let's go!"—a shriek from Betty Lou. Marlon Brando looked rather alarmed. She clumped his sides encouragingly with her sandaled feet. Mr. Brando coughed demurely, but did not move.

"My camels go only when I say," said the shiny brown gentleman. I got a silly impression he would whisk us quickly into unexplored desert territory and hold us for ransom. I dismissed this as arrant nonsense, but the thought remained at the back of my head. The guide said "*arrrghhhuupp*" or something like that, and the caravan of beasts lumbered obediently forward.

After five minutes of the soft swaying motion, I could bear it no longer.

"Zasu Pitts, stop!" I ordered.

The guide was agitated. "What is it? What is the matter?"

"You British!" Betty Lou sniffed.

"Let me down. Let me off," I demanded.

"A long way yet."

"The smell." I waved my hand vaguely as I

dismounted. "This camel smells to high heaven."

"No, no, a lovely camel. This is an insult." The guide was fierce, his eyes ablaze.

"The insult is to Zasu Pitts," I replied. "She, or rather this camel, smells like nine open drains. I can't go any further until I spray her."

"Spray her?" The shiny brown gentleman was bewildered.

"Yes," I said, "I am rarely without my Blue Grass." (This was untrue but sounded good. I had bought a bottle of Blue Grass perfume that morning in the market as a gift to be sent to my mother.)

I unzipped my P&O bag and sprayed the animal lavishly. I even sprayed the shiny brown gentleman. It made him shine even more, I noticed. "Pooh!" he said, waving the cologne away.

"Nonsense," I reprimanded him. "Elizabeth Arden, the manufacturer of Blue Grass, would not like to hear you say that."

Then suddenly, without warning, Zasu Pitts went berserk. She reared and kicked and jigged an animated circle, as though trying to shake the invisible mist from her skin. (Also in need of Arden care—moisturizer—I noted absently.)

"My camel! My camel!" shrilled the guide.

"Heavens!" cried Betty Lou, her cine camera whirring, recording the event for friends back in Memphis, Tennessee.

Marlon and all the other camels watched Zasu with sympathy, except for one named Joan Crawford, who seemed strangely pleased. Then in a flurry of contortions, Zasu Pitts groaned and fell over—dead!

"You owe me lots of money. My most expensive camel!" the guide screamed. Quite crafty of him, I thought.

"Gee," said Betty Lou still whirring, "Myrt just

won't believe this."

Nor did Elizabeth Arden when I wrote her.

"Anyway," Arden's letter in reply to mine finished, "I do not make cosmetics for camels."

An oversight.

CHAPTER TWELVE

A Surprise Meeting

The camel story when published led to others, which today would not be the case with its implicit ethnic slurs. However, it was a different time and in the hope I do not offend, and in the spirit of keeping the record straight, that was what I wrote and what was published.

Later articles of mine appeared in *Time & Tide, Spectator, Harper's Bazaar, Woman's Own,* and a magazine called *Man About Town*, which became *About Town* and then *Town,* and when it had nowhere else to go, it went out of business.

I earned a small reputation as "Firbankian" (I had to look it up, and suggest you do, too).

This new occupation of mine—writing—led to a better class of parties than those I had attended as a filing clerk.

At one of these—a dinner thrown by an even more fey writer than myself, Beverly Nichols—I found myself seated next to Peter Arne, a fairly well known actor of the period. I recognized him from his many TV appearances. A regular on *The Avengers* and *Prisoner* series, Peter was also reportedly a friend of Noël Coward.

Gathering my courage, I approached him. "I hear you know Noël Coward."

"Slightly," he answered. His cool, reserved manner told me he was not going to gossip.

"I would like to meet him more than anything else in the world."

"Aren't I enough?" Peter smiled a dashing, dangerous smile.

I melted.

Our knees touched, our eyes met, we exchanged smiles and phone numbers, and within days, we were between crisp, white sheets. We became, for a time, what society columnists of the period would call "an item," except it was pre-Wolfenden times and was still a "love that dare not speak its name." And so rather than "an item," I guess our coupling would be better described as a "crime."

One night, as I was writing a Firbankian piece for *Queen* magazine, my phone rang. It was Peter who said it had been a bad day for him. Down to two actors for a BBC TV series, the producers had chosen the other actor. Rejection is as much a part of an actor's daily repertoire as showering, but they never seem to acclimatize themselves to this. (The rejection that is, not the showering.)

"I am very depressed," Peter said in a very depressed voice. "Could you come over as soon as possible?"

"I have an article for *Queen* that I have to finish," I said with an air of braggadocio. "But I'll be through with it in about ten minutes."

The article was an interview with the British film actress Diana Dors, on what makes her happy and what makes her unhappy. What made her happy were "theater, sex, travel, and money." And what made her unhappy were "theater, sex, travel, and money."

I assured Peter that as soon as I was through with this capricious piece, I needed a shower and shave and so would be there within an hour.

"Forget the shower, forget the shave," Peter cried woefully, "I need company."

"Okay," I replied. It was early in our relationship,

and I was forthcoming in these matters, which would become far too frequent and eventually destroy the friendship.

I was at Peter's door in a flash.

When he greeted me, he said with a sly smile, "In between phoning you and your arrival, two friends have dropped by."

Having skipped the shave and shower, I panicked. "I can't meet anyone looking like this," I demurred. Stubble, T-shirt, and jeans were not in fashion in those days and even when they did become fashionable, it was a look that never suited me.

"Don't be silly," Peter purred. "I've told them all about you, and they are dying to meet you."

I was apprehensive but followed him into his small, cozy, bric-a-brac filled drawing room. Standing in front of a fire, with their backs to me, were two sartorially elegant gentlemen.

One turned around. It was Dirk Bogarde. He was a big movie star at the time, and I was knocked out.

Then the other gentleman also turned, only this time my heart stopped. It was Noël Coward!

Struck with awe, aware and ashamed of my stubble, my coffee stained T-shirt, and dirty jeans I stuttered, "It's like coming face to face with God!"

"How very reassuring," Noël Coward replied. "I have always been a little terrified of that gentleman and if he is as kind and thoughtful as I am, then I need have no fear."

I sat at his feet for an hour, adoring him openly, listening as he told of the difficulties he was having with the Savoy (both the hotel and theater) and the fact that he was having no difficulties with Elaine Stritch, who was making her London debut in his new musical *Sail Away*.

(Peter irreverently called it, *Piss Off!*)

Coward continued by saying how much he admired Joe Layton, who was doing the choreography for his musical, and Grover Dale, a dancer in the show who he said was a knockout (all gay boys in London were aware of Grover and in thorough agreement with The Master's assessment). Peter Matz had made miraculous orchestrations, he said, but what a pity it was about "poor Evelyn." I never learned who poor Evelyn was. Still, I hung on every word.

I watched Coward as if I were to be struck blind and he was to be my last sight. I would remember everything. I noted his mannerisms, head slightly cocked, a pleased smile when he made a humorous remark, the elegance with which he flicked ash from his ever-present cigarette, the Cartier bracelet that circled his wrist, the way he adjusted the knot of his necktie, the red carnation in his buttonhole.

He was his own self-invention, and I appreciated both the art and the artifice of the man. He sensed this and in turn, I think, appreciated me. He laughed a couple of times when I made a bon mot.

I wanted to tell him how he had affected my life, inspired me to leave New Zealand. But I thought better of it. I feared it would make me sound stupid, too like a "fan."

When it came time for Bogarde and Coward to leave, Dirk who had been watching our exchange with interest, remaining mostly silent throughout the evening, said to me, "I am sure people often say to you, 'You are a very Noël Coward sort of person.'"

"As often as they say to Mr. Coward that he is a very Michael Menzies sort of person," I responded.

Bogarde laughed.

Coward waved his hand in the air and said, "I heard that, dear boy! Touché, touché!" and exited the room, Peter's home, and my life, all before I could tell him how hugely he had impacted me.

Then Peter embarked on a furious rant concerning the actor who had been cast in the role Peter believed was his for the asking.

I pretended to listen to him and say, "There, there, everything will be all right. The producers will soon realize their mistake and get rid of the other actor and ask you to take over." (They didn't, and he didn't.) But all I could think about was that I had met Noël Coward.

The rush, the excitement of meeting The Master, being in the same room as he, breathing his rarefied air, having him speak directly to me, eye contact established, stayed with me.

I couldn't sleep. I couldn't work. I could do nothing but hug the memory of that meeting to myself for weeks afterwards. My mind was spinning. The things I had left unsaid, the questions I had failed to ask. Would I ever meet him again?

But none of that mattered for the evening was perfect just as it happened. I wouldn't have changed a thing.

CHAPTER THIRTEEN

Night of Nights

After seven years in London, including having secured my goal of meeting Noël Coward, it seemed the right time to return to New Zealand and see Clive and Mary and the rest of the family.

I was now approaching my twenty-ninth year. Weekly letters between Mary and me had kept the family advised of my doings and travels.

I am sure I had painted a picture that presented me as a young sophisticate moving in elevated circles with a full engagement book and confidante/friend to the famous. Partly true, partly fiction. Mostly fiction. In fact, my life had begun to echo Marlene's stage performances: illusion, smoke, and mirrors. I was in reality just getting by.

I had planned a ten-day stay in New Zealand with visits to each of my siblings and a big family lunch as a sort of grand finale. At the family lunch there were eighteen of us, more or less, as my sibling's children kept running around, and I may have counted some twice and some not at all.

Mary was beaming like a lighthouse: she had always wanted to preside over a full family dinner and my absence had prevented this. Now she had her wish and watching her made my heart glad.

My last night in New Zealand was spent with Clive and Mary at their flat. (My sister, her husband, and children had taken over the family house in which I had grown up.) I was to leave early the following morning.

There was an air of love in the room, which prompted me to say, "If there's anything you have ever wanted to ask me now is the time to do so. Except my age," I added, wittily, I thought.

"Don't get me wrong," Mary began, "we love you despite the fact you are homosexual…"

My first reaction was surprise, but I could see she was serious and I sensed that I had to address the moment carefully. I know she felt she had some responsibility for my homosexuality. If only she had breast-fed me as she did my siblings, perhaps I would be married with children on the way. (She was inclined to blame herself for things totally outside her control.)

I was gentle in my reply. "You don't love me despite the fact I have blue eyes or brown hair. I did not choose to be homosexual. ("Gay" meant festive in those days, hence our use of the word "homosexual.")

This exchange sparked a spirited conversation of many things that night, starting with how I had shattered them when I ran away from home at age fifteen and was missing for almost a week. They spoke of their worried days, their sleepless nights. I reddened—I had never fully thought how this had affected them. After all, they seemed happy when I had returned home. Wasn't that the end of it? Wasn't that enough? Didn't that make everything all right?

I countered with how I felt they had overlooked me in favor of my siblings, who were happy to be in New Zealand, and played rugby, and went to nun-chaperoned dances at Saint Benedict's Church hall on Saturday nights. And how Clive had never come to see me as a preacher or a Chinaman or a Gestapo or a hussar or a scorned lover or even as an ant in any of the plays in which I had appeared.

"I came to see you in Kumeu," he replied.

Mary, who was always prepared to cry, and had a

handkerchief scrunched up in her hand, excused herself—I imagine to replace the handkerchief, which throughout the evening had undergone more scrunching than the faces of children receiving vaccinations.

I took advantage of her absence to ask Clive a question that had been on my mind during this visit.

I asked if he resented being Mary's nurse, for that is how I saw their current relationship: he cooked for her, ran her bath, fed her, bought the Heard's Hard Toffee (even hammering it into bite-size pieces for her), changed her library books, as well as making endless cups of tea with two digestive biscuits on the saucer.

He smiled at the question, as though I had said something quite daft and answered, "I don't think of myself as her nurse. Your mother gave me so much pleasure when we were young that if this is the way I have to repay her for all the joy she gave me, then it is no hardship. It is, in fact, my pleasure."

His answer charmed me.

But I surprised myself when I realized that I still had more resentment to get out. It was now or never. I mentioned an occasion that had haunted me all my life and for which I had unresolved ill feelings that had never left me.

Clive had a boat—a motor launch, which he said he bought for the family to enjoy. Mary disliked it intensely. Her bed was her life, her haven, her safe place. The boat afforded her no privacy. Even after all of the children were of an age to refuse holidaying with Clive on his boat, he kept it for another twenty years. So I think he bought it more for himself than the family, but he was a kind man, and perhaps he did buy it for us.

Mary returned with a new handkerchief in her hand. I always thought of these as her "Oh, Lord!" moments.

The incident that had been a thorn in my side for

years was connected to Clive's boat, called *Menai* after the Welsh shipyard where it had been built. On the day this incident occurred, all the children were ashore except for me. I was in my cabin reading. I could not see nor was I seen by the adults who were in the cockpit at the stern of the boat. Boating friends of my parents enjoying beer and laughter and sun.

Sound travels on water, and it wasn't long before I heard the conversation of Clive and Mary and their friends. They were discussing their children, and no one knew I was aboard.

I put my book down and listened keenly to their talk. I agreed with Les Welch's assessment of his offspring. "Not very bright but good kids," he proclaimed.

Then Clive mentioned me. My ears went up like a pointer dog. "Michael can be very amusing at times but it's a shame about his looks. He is so awkward looking."

A knife through the heart! The child of Coward and Dietrich? I was fourteen at the time of this conversation. At that age I felt I was mysterious and glamorous (like Dietrich) and elegant and witty (like Coward). I was truly, deeply hurt. Awkward looking? How could that be?

I never forgot Clive's offhand remark, and I took it to mean it is better to be attractive than amusing. And so began a lifetime of putting exterior beauty ahead of interior beauty. This lead to a rocky and quite spotty romantic life for me. Not Clive's fault that I was listening.

My father was surprised, perhaps even shocked, to hear this story, which I shared with them on this, the last night of my trip. He had no recollection of it, but admitted it had the ring of truth, that it was quite likely that he had said it.

"You *were* awkward looking," he confessed.

64

"Most boys of fourteen are."

I laughed. It was true. In an instant, tension disappeared. A long discussion followed, late, past all our bedtimes.

What I heard that night and what I learned was that Clive and Mary did their best for me as they did their best for all their children. And how can one blame anyone for doing his or her best?

It was a revelation to me—all the long-held resentments I had stored up over the years were absurd. I had carried them inside of me, brewing nastily away. Everything Clive and Mary had done for me was done out of love and in the rock-solid belief that it was for the best.

Clive reached over and put his huge, rough yachtsman's hand over mine and said, "Son, this is the night of nights. We had always hoped one of our children would talk to us like this."

Light was beginning to creep into the sky. In a few hours I would be leaving New Zealand.

When it came time to say goodbye—a moment I had dreaded since arrival for I thought another farewell would be like tearing flesh. Strangely, no, it was the easiest goodbye of my life, for we had left nothing unsaid.

Unconditional love.

CHAPTER FOURTEEN

London and New York

While I was in New Zealand, Harper's Bazaar had printed a series of interviews I conducted with various celebrities about things people hated, cunningly titled "Anti-Dotes." "What restaurant do you loathe?" "What book did you hate?" "What film did you walk out of?" Questions like that.

An old-school actor named Sir Donald Wolfit took huge umbrage at a pre-*Phantom of the Opera* Michael Crawford referring to him as "hammy," in the course of one of my interviews.

Lawsuits and horsewhipping were threatened, lawyers consulted, futures in jeopardy, but like most storms in a teacup, it soon evaporated.

I often wondered had the case gone to court how Wolfit would have proved his career had been injured by the word "hammy," as it was a common comment in the reviews of his work.

Nevertheless on my return to London, I found editors wary of me. The Wolfit incident perhaps, or just the changing times? My fey magazine pieces were being rejected in place of writers more in sync with the swinging sixties and the sexual revolution that had just begun. I was out of fashion before I'd come into fashion.

Coward was now a tax exile and spent minimal time in London, while Dietrich was traveling the world with her concertizing, so the likelihood of crossing paths with them in London was less and less. I rationalized to myself that although I had met Coward, I had not yet met Dietrich and somehow I couldn't rest until I had met both my "parents." Make-believe still seemed so right to me.

So I went to New York City, a place both Coward and Dietrich haunted. It was, like most of my life-altering decisions, made impulsively and without much thought and certainly without any planning. I found a rent-controlled apartment in the East Seventies and began to look for work.

Through a series of friends I met Bill Graham (not the evangelical crusader, but the rock and roll promoter), who was in the process of setting up Fillmore East, an old theater in Alphabet City, then a sleazy area and a downtown hippie hangout. It was here that he would present ear-splitting concerts against a zig-zaggy light show featuring artists such as Janis Joplin, Jefferson Airplane, The Who, Credence Clearwater, and many other headliners. He had had immense success offering similar fare at the Fillmore Theater in San Francisco and wanted to repeat that success in New York, a much more cosmopolitan city.

I didn't fit in Bill Graham's world. I wore suits. And underwear. I used 4711 Eau de Cologne. I never said "groovy" nor did I wear love beads.

I was surprised Graham liked me. He definitely had a perverse streak to him because he said, "I'd like you to work for me."

"Doing what?" I asked

"I dunno," he replied off-handedly. "You make me laugh. Not many people do. Just hang out and find something you can do."

So I hung out, a sort of court jester, and although I never found anything significant that I could do, I did a few odd jobs here and there, helped in the box office on occasion, filed in the accounting department, and made myself useful wherever I could. As long as I didn't get dirty.

While Graham was attracting flower children and scruffy hippies to his hip concerts downtown, the great impresario Sol Hurok rented the Metropolitan Opera House uptown each summer when the Opera was *en vacance*. He would present major attractions such as the Royal Ballet, the Stuttgart Ballet, Mosieyev Dancers, and other companies of that stature.

One problem Hurok had in renting the Met was that whatever attraction he had playing there, Sunday nights were always dark, due of course to union rules. But Hurok paid rent for seven days. If he could only find something to fill the Opera House on Sunday nights, he would be in clover: extra income to offset the rent.

Smelling the money Graham was making at the Fillmore East, Hurok suggested that he present Graham's artists at the Met on Sunday nights.

Hurok said, "Think Janis Joplin on the same stage as Maria Callas, Renata Scotto, and Joan Sutherland…" His voice trailed off, unable to choose the correct verb to describe what Joplin did. Hurok wasn't versed in verbs.

Graham was intrigued. It was a good idea, classy even, but he couldn't resist asking, "Renata who?"

They discussed the proposal at length. The two of them talked, they argued, they shouted, both enjoying negotiation, but alas, the idea came to nothing. It all fell apart over a matter of billing. Both men had egos so vast they could only be viewed from the air.

Hurok wanted billing that read "S. Hurok presents Bill Graham's artists at the Met…" whereas Graham would only be satisfied with "Bill Graham in association with S. Hurok presents…"

So what could have been a very interesting, provocative, and even an immensely profitable partnership fell apart before any agreement had been reached. All over a matter of billing. Not for the first time, and certainly not the last time.

But for me it was a wonderful opportunity. "What you do in this dirty place anyway?" Hurok asked reasonably enough. "Come work for me." I was quite ready to leave the druggy, noisy, hippie atmosphere of the Fillmore East for the more subdued air of an office whose clients included Rudolf Nureyev, Maria Callas, Artur Rubinstein, Isaac Stern, Vladimir Ashkenazy, and Mstislav Rostropovich.

"What am I to do?" I asked Mr. Hurok.

"I don't know. You find something."

It was Bill Graham all over again.

I spent the next seven years finding something to do at Hurok Concerts, Inc. As with Graham, I helped in the subscriptions department, filed in the accounting office, greeted VIPs at the Met, and did other odd jobs.

Once Hurok persuaded the Minister of Culture in the Soviet Union, Madame Furtsova, I believe, to allow him to present the Bolshoi Opera and Ballet in the same season. A coup! A dream come true for Hurok.

The announcement in the newspapers of the Bolshoi's New York engagement prompted a scruffy band of political activists known as the Jewish Defense League to protest Hurok's involvement with the Soviet Union at a time when Russia was persecuting the Jews by refusing them permission to emigrate to Israel and generally making life difficult for them.

In frustration and anger at this treatment of Russian Jews, the Jewish Defense League set an incendiary device in the lobby of the Hurok offices timed to explode at 9:30 on the morning of January 26, 1972. And explode it did, on the twentieth floor of the Capitol Records building at Fifty-sixth Street and Sixth Avenue, where the Hurok offices were located. It set off a fire that melted typewriters and cut off exits for staff members, including myself, who had arrived punctually for work at 9:00.

A lesson learned: always be a little late when reporting to the office.

The air conditioning units in the offices acted as ducts for the smoke, and I passed out, gulping for oxygen that was not there. I awoke in hospital that afternoon, surrounded by nurses asking me my name. I tried to tell them, but my throat was a bubble of fire and I could not speak. Someone asked if I was Michael Menzies. I nodded madly, and they all went away, now that they knew who I was.

The next morning the *New York Times* had a picture of me on the front page, being carried out of the building where Hurok had his offices. The caption under the photograph read: "Unidentified Woman on a Stretcher."

I instantly grew a mustache.

Mr. Hurok was devastated by the incident. It was his belief, and one I shared, that people who danced and sang together are less likely to fight. He truly believed that he was doing something that encouraged international peace. But the wind was whisked from his sails and it wasn't long before he died, depressed and beaten.

Hurok Concerts was sold and the firm staggered on until 1977, when it simply whimpered and died too, like its founder. Mr. Hurok had set up his concert business so that it would not outlast him. His gifts were the devotion and care he showed his clients, his contracts guaranteeing them his individual guidance and advice, and without him there to personally guide them, the artists soon went elsewhere.

This meant I had to go, too.

Without formal education and with a rag bag of a "career," including filing, writing fey magazine pieces, and odd jobbing in the music business, there was only one place for me to go: the film industry. At least, I consoled myself, it was an arena in which Coward and Dietrich both had had major success, so it was a connection of sorts, however tenuous.

I remained their devoted child.

CHAPTER FIFTEEN

Firefly

In 1978, at age forty-three, I was hired by the newly formed Orion Pictures, a breakaway group from United Artists. I was to be their financial representative, a job for which I had neither the necessary background nor the abilities, but that didn't seem to trouble anyone.

I learned very soon that it was really a non-job with few duties, countersigning checks and phoning Orion executives from film locations to tell them what was going on: "Two days behind schedule" or "Wardrobe budget gone over by $30,000," that sort of thing. And so it fitted my requirements neatly: very little work for which I was paid handsomely. They seemed pleased with me, and I was certainly pleased with them.

In 1983, I was assigned to a film entitled *Harry & Son.* Starring husband and wife team Paul Newman and Joanne Woodward, the movie was directed by Paul, doing double duty as actor and director. Robby Benson was the "& Son."

Considering the star power connected with this movie, there were high hopes for it, which sadly were never realized. High hopes for Orion Pictures were similarly dashed when they went bankrupt while still in infancy.

However, it was during the filming of this movie, which was at a theater near you for less than a week, that I met the man who would become my life-partner, Eduardo de la Grana. I had grandly rented a yacht to live on during the film shoot in Fort Lauderdale. It had two staterooms, and so I wrote to friends inviting them to join me on my yacht and sample the delights of South Florida.

Many accepted my invitations, among them a young designer friend from New York named Marc Feld.

On the Saturday morning of Marc's visit, I had made coffee and was sipping it pensively in the cockpit when Marc made an appearance. "I brought someone back last night," he told me. "He's still below deck, sleeping."

"Hustle him off the boat as soon as you can," I replied dismissively. "I am not in the mood to meet anyone today."

This was true. I had woken up out of sync for no discernable reason. I felt like one of those comic books where the color bleeds, the lips becoming part of the cheek.

"I really want you to meet him," Marc insisted. "Talking with him last night, I thought to myself, this is a person Michael would enjoy. You have so much in common: love of the theater, wanderlust to the extreme, an appreciation of all the fine things in life."

"*Hmmm*," I thought, curiosity piqued.

I handed Marc a Polaroid camera.

"Take his picture," I said, "and if I like what I see, I will ask him to join us for coffee."

Marc did as he was bid and returned with two Polaroid pictures.

The first one was of an extremely handsome, tanned young Cuban asleep. The second was of the same young man sitting up, a startled look on his face, awakened presumably by the Polaroid flash.

"Ask him how he likes his coffee," I told Marc and went down to the galley to make a fresh pot.

And that is how Eduardo de la Grana came into my

life. Marc was right: we do have a lot in common, and we have remained one another's family for nigh on thirty years.

I learned over coffee and Danish on that Saturday morning that Eduardo and his family had fled Cuba in 1968, under an agreement entered into by the United States and Cuba. President Lyndon B. Johnson had something to do with it. The Great Society. Or the Beautification of America. (This is not a history lesson, so bear with me.) The family settled in Miami where Eduardo learned English watching a TV program called *That Girl* (Marlo Thomas was That Girl).

Trips to New York staying at the Plaza Hotel (Eduardo certainly knew how to travel first class) and visits to the theater had solidified a love of plays, concerts, opera, and ballet, which remain with him to this day.

Getting to know him on the boat we played "Bests."

"Best play?" I asked him.

"Streetcar Named Desire," he answered without a pause.

"Best Actress?" he volleyed back at me.

"Zoe Caldwell in *Medea,*" I replied promptly.

"Me, too!" he shot back. "I was at her last performance—a Sunday matinee."

"That's when *I* saw her!" I marveled.

When he was eighteen years old, Eduardo had seen Dietrich in concert. "I thought she had a nerve," he said. "I didn't know who she was but all the gay boys in Miami were going and could talk of nothing else. So I went, too. She looked magnificent, but she couldn't sing. She stood still, hardly moved at all and sounded foghorny. I wondered what all the fuss was about. And then the curtain calls! Suddenly I knew what all the fuss was about. I fell in love with her."

Eduardo was twenty-seven when I met him, and it was rare to find a man of his age who even knew who Dietrich was. He knew and loved Donna Summer, Grace Jones, Stevie Nicks, and surprise of surprises, he knew and loved Marlene Dietrich, too. He was a prize. I had to add him to my life, where he remains to this day, still a prize.

Perhaps he knew of Noël Coward?

"Yes," he said, "I saw his play called *Noël Coward in Two Keys*. It starred Jessica Tandy, who was the original Blanche du Bois in *Streetcar Named Desire*," he added knowingly.

A beautiful young man who knew of my world, who shared its pleasures and knew its denizens! We talked and talked, names tumbling over one another, vast areas of trivia that I shared with no on else.

He had to leave to go to his job at Air Florida, which granted him free travel for himself and a guest. ("It's called a buddy pass," he explained to me.)

I later learned that he had written in his diary of our meeting: "I met Hermione Gingold on her yacht this morning!"

I found a note on my pillow when I was preparing for bed later that night. It read: "I could have danced all night" and it was signed "Eduardo" followed by his phone number.

I phoned him straight away. None of this waiting two days as advised by Ann Landers. Instant gratification was called for.

Eduardo offered me a buddy pass for the next weekend. We would go to Jamaica to visit the house Noël Coward had lived and died in, and where he was buried.

The first house Coward owned in Jamaica, at Port Santa Maria, was on the water. It was comfortable and unremarkable. He named it Blue Harbor. It was there that guests stayed and communal meals were served. High on a hill above Blue Harbor, Coward built Firefly, which was his own private domain. It was where he wrote, where he composed, where he painted, and in the evenings guests would join him there to watch rainbows and sunsets and enjoy cocktails as swarms of fireflies that gave the house its name lit the darkening sky.

He had died ten years before our visit. Quite suddenly, and one hopes, without pain, having said goodnight to his "family"—partner Graham Payn and right-hand man Cole Lesley—and sent them down to Blue Harbor while he settled in for the night at his beloved Firefly. He had had a heart attack early in the morning, and by the time the gardener had found him and alerted "the boys," he had passed away.

Eduardo and I flew into Montego Bay and took a car to a place called Ocho Rios, where we had booked a hotel room at the Sans Souci.

The night sky was spectacular: black velvet dotted with stars like a Tiffany tray of diamonds. We dined, we talked, we drank crème de menthe frappes. We swam. We were enchanted with the night and with one another. It remains in my memory as one of the most glamorous nights of my life.

The next day we took a hotel car to Firefly.

It was now the property of the Jamaican government and supposedly a tourist spot. Nevertheless no one was there but Eduardo and me. And a guide, full of misinformation.

He started the "tour" by telling us, "This is the room that inspired Coward to write his song 'A Room with A View.'"

"Nonsense!" I replied. "Coward wrote that song in the twenties, and he did not build this house until the fifties."

The guide withdrew. "You know too much more

than me," he said sheepishly and allowed us the freedom to explore the house alone, while he disappeared. He stayed out of sight in the shadows until we left.

Firefly, unlike Blue Harbor, was a one bedroom home, rather plain but very comfortable. The sort of place where you could put bare feet up on tables and sofas without fear of damaging them. It had a sweeping view of the bright blue Caribbean Sea and tropical forests with sudden bursts of color. Birds? Flowers? It didn't matter. There was no one or anything else in sight.

The actress Lynn Fontanne said it reminded her of a matinee audience. "Too many empty seats," she sighed, looking at the view as though scanning the stalls at a mid-week matinee.

It was here that Coward entertained the Queen Mother when she made a trip to Jamaica. They were jolly friends. The salmon prepared for Her Majesty was ruined—had to be thrown out—and cold soup was hastily prepared as a substitute. Wine and liquor replaced pomp. Everyone, including the Queen Mother, got slightly tipsy and had a rip-roaring good old time.

The walls of Firefly held the laughter, the music, and talk that had ricocheted throughout the house—if you listened very carefully, you could almost hear echoes of it. Love and friendship and goodwill had been the currency of this house. Eduardo and I felt it intuitively.

Since we were the only visitors at the time and had been left alone, we sat on the bed that Coward had died in. Eduardo tried on Coward's spectacles that were on a bedside table on top of a Trollope novel. I photographed him wearing them.

We sorted through half completed paintings leaning against the wall that Coward had started and never finished. We sat at his piano and I picked out a little of "I'll See You Again."

Coward was buried here in a grave under a gazebo-type structure at the spot where he would survey his world, alone or with friends, at sunset. Where the fireflies that gave the house its name would dance and fly and sparkle.

We sat in silence at the graveside.

Someone had left flowers.

We waited for the appearance of the fireflies as night fell and tranquility settled over the site. When they appeared, they were very bright, very comforting—like old friends.

With Eduardo at my side, I felt I had come home.

CHAPTER SIXTEEN

Marlene Approaching Sixty

Dietrich was fifty-nine years of age when she met him in 1961.

He was thirty-four; twenty-five years her junior and on the brink of international fame as the star of the widely distributed Polish art film *Ashes and Diamonds*. His name was a tongue twister: Zbigniew Cybulski. No wonder she called him Spishek.

They met in Paris at a big party, locked eyes across the room, and exchanged secret smiles. She learned that he was known as the James Dean of Poland. He hated this comparison, but the similarities in both looks and style could not be denied.

He was a very intense young man; dark, nervous, shy, anguished, and bisexual. Onscreen he was both powerful and authoritative, but offscreen and offstage he always hid behind tinted glasses, an idiosyncrasy he adopted for the character he played in *Ashes and Diamonds*.

Despite spotting one another almost immediately, Dietrich and Cybulski delayed talking to each other, allowing the ebb and flow of the guests to bring them together. Electricity! Sparks! Anticipatory excitement rushed through each person—their body language predicting the yearning and fierce, all-consuming passion that lay ahead for both of them.

Their affair started shortly after their meeting.

Dietrich had acquired an apartment at 12 Avenue Montaigne, off the Champs Elysées, and she invited him

79

up for drinks. (They were both on their way to becoming world-class tipplers.) It was she who asserted herself sexually, and he complied willingly. The love making for both was electric.

She went on record as saying he was "the kindest, the most beautiful man in the world. He was so beautiful that every time I see his photograph, I cry, the kind of man any woman would love, a God!"

He was in Paris appearing onstage in the play *Le thé à la menthe* in what could be called a cameo. Dietrich, ever the perfectionist when it came to matters artistic, ran lines with him. They also attended a Piaf concert at the Paris Olympia—one of a few public appearances they made together.

It is not without significance that Dietrich and Piaf had had their own clandestine affair. Marlene felt entitled to many things lesser mortals were denied, among them the right to have numerous love affairs with both sexes. It was her often stated belief that it was totally acceptable for "great actresses like Sarah Bernhardt" (and presumably herself) to accept love and admiration from any source.

Other than the Piaf concert, the lovers kept a low profile and met mostly at her apartment. In fact, for the run of his play in Paris he moved in with her. However, Cybulski felt being seen publicly with Dietrich would only bring attention to their age difference and somehow injure his career.

"Nonsense," she told him in no uncertain terms. "On the contrary, being seen with me would only rebound to your credit and certainly to your benefit. I am, after all, a major star!" People would take notice and the reflection of her fame on Cybulski could only help his career. Hurt him? How could it hurt him?

Their busy schedules left little time for the affair to truly blossom. It lasted six years after their initial meeting and engrossed them. The age difference went either unnoticed or at least unrecorded. Dietrich was right about that.

Whereas Cybulski had seen numerous Dietrich films and was well aware of her worldwide celebrity, she had seen none of his. Marlene wanted to see Cybulski onscreen. He arranged the screening of one of his early films for her. (English title: *Night Train.* Polish title: forget it! There are no vowels.) The climax of the film had him falling to his death beneath the wheels of a moving locomotive, a scene that haunted Dietrich.

She would awake from a night's sleep, thrust into anxiety when she dreamt about the film sequence. She would then be forced to take another "Fernando Lamas," the name she gave suppositories that acted as sedatives and without which she could never fall asleep. She named them Fernando Lamas as she thought Lamas was the most boring actor she had ever met. "He put me to sleep," she explained simply.

Cybulski on the other hand represented life and excitement and the obsessive sex that was always fueled for them both by alcohol. She followed him to the Edinburgh Festival where he was appearing. His celebrity on the rise, her sexual desire demanding release.

Friends of Cybulski kept Dietrich advised of his doings when they were apart. She was alarmed to learn from them that when she was not around he drank more and more and began to put on weight. She was surprised at his intensity but proud and delighted that her presence, and for that matter, her absence fed it.

It was a foregone conclusion that when she arranged a concert tour that would take her behind the Iron Curtain they would meet in his native Warsaw. She anticipated their reunion with giddy excitement. A young girl in the throes of her first love.

81

On arrival at the airport in Warsaw, she was distressed to find he was not among those waiting to greet her. But at her hotel, now the Bristol Le Meridien but then just the Bristol, there was a handful of messages and phone numbers where he could be found. They all pleaded for her to "call the moment you arrive."

Since so much of their life together was behind closed doors, I imagine that first she bathed in water fragranced by tuberoses and chose a particularly fetching negligee before phoning him. He was there in a flash—their reunion eager and passionate. Their temperaments fitted one another like the last diamond placed in a tiara.

They both possessed extraordinary drive and ambition. If anything, his passion and need for her was greater than the reverse. She had the power and held the control. She would live until ninety before giving it up.

His shyness about being seen with her in public faded, and he attended every one of the six performances she gave in Warsaw, even bringing flowers onstage and proffering them to her at the final concert. He was totally besotted.

Cybulski accompanied her when she laid a wreath at the memorial commemorating the Warsaw uprising of 1944, and she allowed him a very special privilege few ever experienced: he was permitted to attend one of her rehearsals.

Her final concert in Warsaw was a highly charged, highly emotional event. So clamorous was the reaction of the audience calling for "More! More!" for encore after encore, that she was forced to repeat songs she had already sung.

That night, on Cybulski's arm, she went to the Café Oczki, where Polish film students had gathered to honor her. In a dizzying exchange of languages—

French, English, German, and with the aid of an interpreter, Polish—she endeared herself to them. In fact, she became so entranced with the youthful students that when one of them offered to play her songs on the tinkly café piano, she gave an impromptu concert, peppered with rounds of vodka. As the evening progressed, so did the boisterous cheers and bravos, not to mention the rounds of vodka.

Perched on Cybulski's shoulders, with his James Dean-like windbreaker around her own shoulders, Dietrich sang through an open window to a cluster of people shivering in the cold, who had gathered outside the café, unable to gain admittance as it was crowded to its limit.

Cybulski came to the airport this time to see her off—she was tearful as she addressed Spishek and the ubiquitous fans who always greeted her arrival and farewelled her on departures. (Where did they come from? How did they learn of her travel arrangements?)

"I don't want to say goodbye," she murmured huskily. She mounted the steps to the plane, turned at the top of the stairs, waved, smiled, threw a kiss, and exclaimed, "This is not goodbye. I will be back, so *au revoir* till the next time!"

The next time was a year later. Cybulski was at the airport to greet her along with the usual bunch of exuberant, excited fans.

After a second Dietrich triumph in Warsaw, Spishek returned to Paris with her for a short but thrilling visit that rarely let them explore the city further than her apartment on the Avenue Montaigne. I can only imagine how they indulged in Olympian lovemaking. Gold medal sex!

Her preference was oral sex. It was called cunnilingus, she had been told. "I thought that was an Irish airline," she is rumored to have answered.

Their time in Paris was short; he had to leave to fulfill film commitments in his native land.

Dietrich became more and more distraught when mutual friends wrote of Spishek's ever-changing moods. He was "desperate" to see her, to be with her, they wrote. She consoled herself in the same manner he did—a steadily increasing consumption of alcohol.

The affair was now in its sixth year—played out in Paris and Poland and other locations, some exotic, others ordinary. Finding unexpected spare time in between concert bookings, Dietrich flew to Wroclaw, Poland, where her beloved Spishek was filming. She was booked into the Hotel Metropol (curiously enough, the name of the hotel in which most of the action of *Ashes and Diamonds* occurs).

She sent word to him that she was at the Metropol, and within a few hours he joined her rapturously. Heady days followed. They seldom left the room.

When all passion was spent, and they were enveloped in an aura of sultry, post-coital cigarette-sharing languor, I picture her running her fingers through his chest hair and telling him she wants to return to Warsaw and that he should come with her.

His film in Wroclaw was not yet finished; he had one short scene left to complete. After a long period of self-questioning, he said, "I will go with you," followed almost immediately by, "No, I must stay here and finish the film."

However, thinking it over some more, perhaps he would go with her, after all.

Then again, perhaps he would stay.

He booked them two Wagon-Lits for the train journey from Wroclaw to Warsaw.

But perhaps he would stay.

His indecision was driving her mad.

At least he accompanied her to the railway station,

still in a whirl of crazy indecision. But once at the railway terminal, he finally decided that he should stay in Wroclaw and finish his film. Later he would join her "anywhere in the world."

Dietrich understood. Professional commitments always came before personal wishes. This was a law by which she lived her life.

They said farewells, and then as if cued by a stage manager, she left him without a backward glance and retired to her couchette and began preparing for the overnight trip to Warsaw.

Cybulski was in torment. He watched the train pull away from the station, and finding it unbearable, intolerable to be parted from her, he jumped aboard the moving train, lost his footing, and in doing so, fell under the wheels. He was killed instantly. Just like the scene from his film *Night Train*. The scene that haunted Dietrich for the last six years. The irony of it would not be lost on her. Art and life were interchangeable.

Although just forty years old, in death he would become a beloved and renowned figure—an icon in his own country, remembered in death as a trailblazer of Polish film and stage. A bust of him is featured to this day as part of a Warsaw cinema mural.

Dietrich was initially unaware of the disaster. When she questioned railway staff about the emergency stop and delay as workers struggled to free her lover's body from beneath the wheels of the train, she was placated by their response of "Signal problems. Do not worry, madame."

On arrival in Warsaw the next morning, she learned of her lover's death from railway officials. Why had she wanted to go there? Was it destiny or just plain bad luck? Unanswered questions that would remain with her for the rest of her days.

She asked the officials if she could be the last to

leave the train. She needed time to compose herself. Of course they agreed.

Reporters in Warsaw were forewarned and asked not to mention Cybulski to her. Amazingly enough, they refrained from asking anything about the actor, and she got through the familiar and tiring pattern of posing for photographs and the endless, senseless questions.

She operated on automatic pilot—her professionalism taking over—the circus horse smelling the sawdust and beginning its routine.

So many of the reporters' questions were ones she had answered over and over on numerous occasions.

"What is the secret of your glamour?"

"Money."

She was now in professional mode. She could not allow her image to be unmasked. No one watching her had any inkling that she was heart-broken. She was Marlene Dietrich: film star, singer, international icon, in total control.

She heard the usual boring questions asked of her, and replied mechanically like a wound up doll.

"Do you like the mini-skirt or do you prefer longer dresses?"

"Fashion bores me. Why don't you ask me about important issues, like what I think of women's liberation?"

"Okay. What do you think of women's liberation?"

"It bores me."

Eventually they let her go.

This love affair was the last one of any length that Dietrich would experience.

Spishek's photo was added to the "wall of death" in her Paris apartment, where friends and lovers who had died were remembered. New ones, it seemed, being added every week, jostling for space on the wall just as they had jostled for space in her life.

Eight more years of what she called "schlepping around the world" were ahead for her. Concerts would be scheduled and performed. Itineraries prepared and booked. She became increasingly cantankerous and short tempered with those around her, and more and more dependant upon alcohol to get through days of airports, nights of entertaining, endless, silly repartee, and different hotel suites that all blurred in memory into one.

For the rest of her life she lived tired—sleep deprived. Even the Fernando Lamases lost their effectiveness.

CHAPTER SEVENTEEN

Noël Approaching Sixty

Unlike Dietrich, Coward had created a family of trusted friends who offered him support, enthusiasm, and unwavering loyalty. Their job was to deal with the minutiae of his life, shielding The Master from petty daily affairs. Sometimes one or other of them would accompany Coward as he traveled around the world, indulging his insatiable wanderlust.

However, his preference was to travel alone, and there is hardly a country in the world that he failed to visit. To underscore his temperament, he wrote a song that became a staple in his cabaret performances: "I Travel Alone."

He was by nature a very curious and inquisitive man. He liked and welcomed new experiences. He found traveling extremely productive. Many of his works were conceived and sometimes written on ships, in foreign lands, isolated beaches, and sometimes in hotels. Travel was also an extremely restorative exercise for him: a cure for the demands of his professional and social lives.

His self-created family consisted of Lorn Loraine, who served as his right-hand for forty-six years; Lesley Cole ("Coley"), hired as a secretary but soon became Coward's indispensable pooh bah; and Graham Payn ("Little Lad"), who at first was Coward's lover then ended up an intimate friend. Theirs was an open and thoroughly honest relationship, both of them enjoying the freedom of choosing others to bed. But ultimately they always came home to one another.

As he was approaching sixty, at almost the same age his friend Dietrich welcomed Cybulski into her life, Coward also had his last fling of any note. It may be a natural reflex as one is approaching sixty—a confirmation that one is still attractive enough to find love.

Nude With Violin, a comedy that Coward wrote in 1954, opened in London two years later to grim notices, but played to near capacity audiences for over eighteen months. ("Only the public seems to like my work," he said sardonically.) John Gielgud was hired to play the leading role – a sinister but utterly charming butler to a famous painter. Gielgud relinquished the role after a year to Michael Wilding, who Coward said brought to the role "a great deal of personal charm, increased audiences, and startling inaudibility." Wilding was later replaced by Robert Helpmann, the actor/dancer whose makeup for the part resembled that of a silent movie star: exaggerated mouth and kohled eyes. A legacy of his ballet days, no doubt, but he carried off the role with stellar success. Another example of Coward overcoming poor critical notices.

For its inevitable New York production, Coward decided he would assume the leading role himself, but to overcome his stage nerves (he had not appeared on Broadway for twenty-one years), he brought over with him many of the London cast.

The Broadway producers were rather surprised when, at the auditions for the lesser parts, Coward, given a choice of six actors for one of the roles, chose the least of the six performers.

However, this odd and out-of-character behavior soon became clear: Coward was deeply attracted to the twenty-seven-year-old, six foot two, dark, dashing, handsome actor. His name was William (Bill) Traylor, and this was his first Broadway engagement.

Coward re-wrote Bill's role (that of an inquiring reporter from *Time* magazine) so that it became more important and pivotal to the play. Since Traylor was at best a workman-like actor, this did not add much to the production. In fact, some felt it detracted from the play's impact.

Traylor had been raised by a strict Catholic family in rural Montana. As one might guess, his family did not encourage his chosen career. Previous stage experience was meager, including summer stock productions and tours. Being chosen by Coward himself was an enormous boost to the young actor's self-esteem and confirmed (incorrectly as it turned out) that he was in the right profession.

At first deeply flattered by Coward's personal interest in him, Traylor grew increasingly alarmed and agitated by its intensity and the intimate direction Noël expected things to go. Bill did everything in his power (other than to resign and walk away) to resist the sexual advances of The Master.

The unlikely coupling of a world famous writer/actor/composer and a struggling, mediocre actor did not go unnoticed by the rest of the company. Everyone connected to *Nude With Violin* was aware of the behind-the-scenes drama waiting to erupt, and an uneasy air fell over the production.

On the street and in the press, there was much excited buzz about Noël Coward's return to Broadway to perform in his new play. Famous actors of the period (Alfred Lunt and his wife Lynn Fontanne, Katherine Cornell, Helen Hayes, Clifton Webb, et al) took out full-page advertisements in various papers and magazines welcoming him back. Theater parties (then the life blood of a new show) displayed great interest and booked performances accordingly.

Coward was sure that all these omens would result in a sure-fire success, but the glum reaction of preview audiences disturbed him.

His fears were realized on opening night. The press was far from kind.

The *New York Herald Tribune* critic Walter Kerr wrote, "It is delightful to have Mr. Noël Coward back in the theater. It would have been more delightful to have him back in a play." Brook Atkinson in the *New York Times* echoed Kerr's displeasure with the production: "The old assurance has gone," he sadly informed his readers.

The reviews hit Coward badly, as though he had been kicked in the stomach.

Unable to do anything to improve the play, he turned to love for consolation. As with most things, he threw himself into it totally and completely. He did not heed his own instincts or take the kind of advice he so breezily offered to others. He knew he was demeaning himself and embarrassing Bill Traylor, but it appeared impossible to untangle himself from the messy arrangement.

Years earlier he had written a poem entitled "I Am No Good at Love." As was his pattern, almost immediately he felt the end of the affair before it had even begun. No good at love indeed. The songs of love he had written over the years would enter his brain, mocking him, never leaving.

With Traylor, Coward displayed an unseemly possessive side. When, for instance, he learned that Bill had made a date with one of the actresses in the company, Coward told the hapless, helpless producers that they had to fire her. They were reluctant to do so, but Coward was coldly insistent.

"Tell her she is too good for the part," he demanded icily.

Further frustration had him lecturing Traylor in his star dressing room. Between a matinee and evening performance, he warned the young actor, "You have to be faithful to me, and if you aren't, make sure I don't know and never find out."

He ranted at Traylor, who was maddeningly silent and unresponsive during this uncharacteristic tirade, which was overheard by many in the company, including Noël's own devoted Coley.

Coward knew the affair was so one-sided that it would inevitably collapse. He knew, too, that Traylor was not attracted to him (or any man for that matter). But in spite of all this, Coward persisted. He forced Traylor to accompany him home, hoping a few after-show drinks would loosen his inhibitions. Their lovemaking was unsatisfactory to both of them, but Coward doggedly demanded that it continue.

The confusion and shame that flooded Coward's mind and heart overrode his instincts and his own advice. Coward was well known for "finger wagging," as he upbraided friends and colleagues alike for their perceived failures. This finger wagging was feared by some, a genuine help to others. Sometimes his counsel was sought out, and sometimes it was ignored, but the finger wagging was a facet of his personality that was a lifelong habit.

"Snap out if it, Viv," he would tell the wildly schizophrenic Vivien Leigh in one of her manic moods, as if this would cure her of her mental instability.

He wished he would not fall in love, but when he did, he could not handle it and berated himself mercilessly. Coward was a highly honest man—his personal and professional ethics without question. He must have felt great shame over this "affair" with Traylor; the fact he was taking advantage of a young man must have caused Noël excruciating torment. He was letting himself down.

It is an indication of Coward's private emotions and inner distress that he was forced to miss performances—five in a row one week. He was plagued with a series of colds and vocal problems. If only he could finger-wag himself.

It appeared that he shared his secret unhappiness with no one. It was only after his death and the publication of his diaries and biographies by eminent Coward scholars, that this dalliance with Traylor was revealed.

It must be noted that in his diaries and letters, Coward was writing for posterity. He never mentioned Traylor by name, despite the passionate obsession he felt. Nor did he mention dates or places connected with the affair. He never liked to paint himself in less than total control. His own personal motto was "Rise above it," but in this instance he was unable to do so. Hence the diary entries for this incident are both vague and ultimately self-serving. A reference to that "ol' black magic" leaves the reader scratching his head and trying to read between the lines.

Despite this self-flagellation, Coward could not help himself. And it seemed as though poor, weak-willed Bill Traylor could not help himself either. They were locked in their unhappy and wretched dance.

One night towards the end of the play's run, Traylor somehow managed to extricate himself from another humiliating night at Coward's apartment and went home to his own place, an apartment in the East Sixties that he shared with a flat mate named Hugh MacMillan.

On arrival at his apartment, Traylor traded hellos with MacMillan and disappeared into the bathroom where he took a slew of sleeping pills and collapsed.

MacMillan heard the fall and rushed to offer aid but he could not revive his friend.

He phoned the producers of the play, as well as Coward, and alerted them to the dire situation. He told them Traylor had returned home quite intoxicated. Coward swore that after a few shared drinks, he and Bill had parted, and the young man appeared "quite fine" to The Master.

MacMillan called the police when he found an empty bottle of Seconal, a strong, potentially lethal sedative. He had tried to revive his roommate, but was unable to do so. An ambulance was summoned, and Traylor was admitted to the nearby Roosevelt Hospital.

Other than an item in the *New York Post* ("Sleeping Pills Fell Actor In Coward Show"), the press ignored the event—testament to the power of the producers and Noël's own lofty position in the theater. No word of Coward's involvement with Traylor was ever published during his lifetime.

In order to keep the lamentable affair from the public, as well as shielding his spotless image, neither Coward nor the producers commented publicly on the incident. Nor is there any record that they offered any assistance, but surely they must have.

As recorded in his posthumously published diaries, Noël confided to Charles Russell, his American business manager, that he visited his tortured friend at Roosevelt Hospital and discovered him in a straightjacket "frothing at the mouth." I am not sure this was true but it made for a colorful story.

This sad occurrence at last ended their sexual dalliance, but strangely, on dismissal from the hospital, Traylor returned to the cast and was even rewarded with a plum role (Roland Maule) in *Present Laughter,* which went into repertory with *Nude With Violin* in an effort to boost the slumping box office at the Belasco Theatre, where both plays were presented in rotation.

Present Laughter is one of Coward's masterpieces, and up to that time had never been performed on Broadway. It is an autobiographical tongue-in-cheek account of an actor/writer and the various complications, lies, and maneuvering necessary to get him through the day. The Master played it to perfection and it certainly served its purpose: wonderful notices and full houses. And thus his last stage appearance on Broadway reaffirmed Coward's reputation as a leading playwright and actor, and he was sent on his way with farewell cheers resonating in his ears.

Traylor had been a member of the Actor's Studio, where Lee Strasberg reigned supreme and imparted his theories of acting known as "the Method," an approach to the art that Coward found particularly suspect.

He once asked actress Maureen Stapleton, "Why do you go? What do you get out of it?"

"It keeps me off the streets," she replied.

"Ah, but Maureen, it's the streets where you belong!"

Although they never kept contact after the closing of *Nude* and *Present Laughter*, Bill Traylor went on to appear in a few more Broadway productions, either as an understudy or in small roles.

Traylor died of undisclosed causes in 1990 as he was approaching the worrying age of sixty.

"Emotion is so very untidy," Coward had once written. He swept the affair with Traylor under the rug and never wrote of it or spoke of it publicly. His image, so carefully guarded, would not be tarnished.

He rose above it.

CHAPTER EIGHTEEN

Me Approaching Sixty

It is only in retrospect that I found my own fifty-ninth birthday brought me to a point in my life that will always remain seminal. To my way of thinking (odd, I must admit), this linked me once more to Dietrich and Coward in some inexplicable way. I was always on the look out for such omens.

I had been in the habit of adding ten years to my age for quite some time. It was in the hope people would look at me and say, "My God, you look terrific for your age!" No one ever did.

However, I persisted with this pretence. I was convinced someone eventually would be amazed and comment on how young I looked for my declared age. I was quite sure this would happen. It never did.

When I met Eduardo I hoped things would change in this regard. During the burgeoning period of our relationship, Eduardo learned from me that I was fifty-nine years old. (I was, in fact, forty-nine.) I wanted to hear him say, "My God, you look good for your age!"

But it didn't happen. Just a disinterested "Really?" and a shocking admission that he was twenty-seven. Shocking because this made me twenty-one years his senior.

When the filming of the Paul Newman vehicle *Harry & Son* was completed in Florida, I returned to New York with Eduardo. I threw a party for all my friends to meet him. I was told by those friends "I give it six months," "He will break your heart," "He will walk all over you." These were the most frequent responses. There was one other: "May I have his telephone number?"

When I told Eduardo about these responses, he said, "It's probably true, but it will be a wonderful six months. You won't want to miss them. And by all means, give the person who asked for it my telephone number."

It has turned into a wonderful thirty years.

When people ask me the secret of a long and happy relationship, I always tell them separate bedrooms, and more importantly, separate bathrooms are the answer. This coupled with the fact that we make each other laugh at least once a day has kept us going and kept us together.

Eduardo is one of those people who never lies— under any circumstances—and it bothered me that I had created a situation where I had to be careful about dates, altering stories of my past so that they were in line with my declared age.

A year later, I blurted out the truth to him. "I am going to be fifty this year," I told him over breakfast.

"You mean sixty," the Cuban replied.

"No, fifty," I repeated. "I lied about my age when we first met."

"Why?"

"So that you would say I look great for my age."

"Did I?"

"No."

"Well it's true—you look more like sixty than you do fifty."

I showed him my passport as proof of my real age.

Rather that being charmed by my thinking process, he was angry. "What else have you lied about? How can I trust you ever again?"

"Most of what I have told you about my life is

true," I replied. "But I do like to embroider the truth, just to make it more interesting. Zero Mostel does the same, and so do many other famous people. Dali, Tallulah Bankhead…" I couldn't think of any others at that moment. (Ask me now and I can give you a list as long and as winding as China's Great Wall.)

"I am not interested in other people. I am interested in you."

I took that as a compliment and assured Eduardo I would never lie to him again. And I have kept my word—with a few exceptions. After all, habits die hard and memory plays cunning tricks. And let's face it; the truth can be very boring.

My point is that without knowing of the romances that had made Dietrich's and Coward's fifty-ninth years so searing and defining, I followed suit with my own. I tied my future to a much younger man, just as they had tried to do. It made my connection with Noël and Marlene stronger, I felt.

My fifty-ninth year was kinder to me than they were to my pretend "parents." They lost Cybulski and Traylor from their lives. I kept Eduardo in mine.

Eduardo's mother continues to believe I am ten years older. "Passports can be altered," she whispered to her son as though she were speaking from behind a fan. "And he looks much older than he claims to be."

I cannot speak Spanish. She cannot speak English. So I cannot convince her otherwise.

CHAPTER NINETEEN
Two Deaths

After the collapse of Orion Pictures, I went to work for Raffaella De Laurentiis, daughter of the legendary producer Dino De Laurentiis, as a production accountant, another job for which I had neither qualifications nor ability. And she paid me well.

I had spoken to Academy Award-winning cinematographer Jack Cardiff about my feelings. I told him I felt like the emperor with no clothes, that I was naked and one day someone would point at me and say, "He doesn't know what he is doing" and that would be the end of me.

"Everyone in movies feels the same way," he replied. "If we didn't, if we knew everything, there would be no such thing as a flop movie. Some people are born beautiful, some are born talented. We," and he included me in his sweep of hand, "are born lucky. To distrust that pattern of luck is an insult to God or whoever it is that rules the universe. He won't suddenly rip the carpet of luck from under your feet. You will always be lucky."

So I began to trust my luck.

Working with the De Laurentiis family was great. They were generous, kind, and caring. They took us to film locations all over the world. At last I understood Coward's maxim that "work is more fun than fun." For the first time in my life, in my fifties, I worked at a real job. I didn't have to find things to do.

Air Florida, like Orion, collapsed and with it

disappeared Eduardo's job and the "buddy" passes. So he came to work for me as my assistant. Many years later on a China Airlines flight from Hong Kong to Beijing, Eduardo pulled at the seat cover and discovered Air Florida's logo underneath. Even China Airlines had come a long way. We all had. The airplane from Florida, Eduardo from Cuba, me from New Zealand.

We were based in Guangzhou (once Canton), China, working on a film called *Tai-Pan*– also at a theater near you for four days.

Producer Raffaella De Laurentiis became alarmed when at breakfast one morning an American businessman, whom she had never met, warned her that the Chinese – no matter what our contract with them stated—were likely to demand taxes when it was time for us to leave the country.

"Probably they will hold your film and equipment as collateral," he told her. "You will never get it out of this country. Corrupt," he explained. He sounded convincing, to Raffaella anyway.

She suggested Eduardo and I over a period of a week smuggle all accounting records out of China into Hong Kong, which was still British territory and therefore not subject to Chinese rules.

Much in the manner of aristocrats fleeing Tsarist Russia with jewels stitched in their skirts, each morning Eduardo and I left China by train, lugging heavy paper-filled suitcases full of files and supplies and anything to do with the accounting records of the film.

China at this time did not believe in servile occupations, so there was no such thing as railway porters, and it was not until arrival in Hong Kong that we could count on any help with our burdensome luggage.

After four days of round trip journeys from China to Hong Kong, we arrived exhausted and weary at the hotel in Hong Kong, where we were to establish the accounting department of *Tai-Pan*.

On arrival at the hotel this particular day, the receptionist handed a sheaf of telephone messages to Eduardo. They were all from Raffaella, and they we all marked "urgent." This was surprising since, although the two of them had a separate, cordial, even loving relationship, normally Raffaella addressed any accounting problems or questions to me.

"What can it mean?" we asked one another, dreading the worst: that we would have to repeat this exercise and return to China. Had the American whose advice Raffaella took at breakfast been discredited?

Eduardo phoned Raffaella. They spoke in Spanish. Despite many years spent with Spanish and Italian-speaking people, I have no ear for language other than English, in which I am quite fluent. When foreign tongues are wagging in my presence, I always feel I am in a bird aviary.

When Eduardo replaced the receiver, he turned to me and said in a shriveled voice, "There is no way to break this to you gently. A fax was received in China this morning after our departure. It was for you, and it was from your sister. Your father died in New Zealand this morning."

"No!" I cried. "Surely you mean my mother?" (*Heard's Hard Toffee had at last taken its toll*, I thought.)

"No, I specifically asked that," Eduardo replied. "It was Clive."

A phone call to my sister confirmed this.

It seemed that on a Friday night, Mary complained of chest pain. Clive called the doctor, and before he arrived, Clive himself began to feel ill. On his arrival, the doctor called for two ambulances and my parents were taken from their flat on gurneys. Carried to separate ambulances, they held hands on their stretchers, letting go of one another only when they were placed in different ambulances and taken to two different hospitals.

They would never see one another again.

Unable to sleep and with only one more Hong Kong/Guangzhou roundtrip ahead to complete our task, I asked Eduardo to set up the office in Hong Kong while I returned to China alone.

Upon arrival in China, there was an urgent message for me to call Eduardo in Hong Kong.

I did so.

"You won't believe it," he stammered. "Almost immediately after you left Hong Kong, another fax arrived from your sister. Your mother died last night."

I recalled that before each family holiday on the boat, Clive would go ahead two days prior, to prepare the boat for Mary's arrival. It seemed to me that even in death, he was doing the same thing: he went two days before her, arranging for Mary's arrival in the next world.

They had always told me, "Please don't come home for our funerals. We want you to celebrate life rather than death." I honored this request and drowned myself in numbers and cost reports and budgets. It kept me occupied. Activity always does.

CHAPTER TWENTY

Dietrich in Paris

Coward had died. Clive and Mary were gone.

There was only Dietrich left.

No longer concertizing, she was now a recluse in her elegantly located apartment on the Avenue Montaigne. With one exception, a last, ill-advised final film appearance, she now passed the rest of her days on the fourth floor of her building.

Her autobiography, *Marlene*, soon appeared: a slight book that rightly belongs in the "fiction" section of libraries and bookstores. (Next to Tallulah Bankhead's account of her own life.) Both ladies determined to bend facts, alter dates, and re-write history. Their lives re-invented to fit the image they had created. Both still in control.

In addition to writing her autobiography Dietrich had consented to allow her extraordinary life and career to be the subject of a feature-length documentary. However, she insisted she would not appear on camera. Stills and clips from her movies and privately shot footage from her personal life, along with an audio interview that she consented to, would have to suffice.

Actor Maximilian Schell, who appeared with Dietrich in her last movie of any distinction, *Judgment at Nuremberg*, agreed to direct the documentary for which Marlene—historically broke—was paid $100,000. Any money form any source at this point of her life was welcome. Her advancing years had caused her to outlive her extravagances and income.

103

Schell came to her Paris apartment with camera crew and equipment, and found her truculent and totally uncooperative. Asked questions about her career and life, she would querulously reply, "I wrote about that in my book. Tell them [presumably the audience watching her documentary] to read my book, they will find the answers there!" Sullenly or drunkenly switching from English to German as it took her fancy, she would even identify where the audience could find the answer. "Page forty-four!" she would snap.

Dietrich, who had controlled all aspects of her professional life up to this point, understood she would not be able to control this film, so perversely she made it impossible for Schell to finish it.

Driven to despair by her lack of cooperation, Schell left after four days of to-ing and fro-ing with her, convinced that he could not complete his assignment. But Schell was Swiss-born and with the stubborn and concrete determination common to the Swiss, decided to make it a documentary about how difficult it was to make a documentary about Marlene Dietrich.

There is a surreal scene of him walking blindly through hanging raw stock, pushing it violently aside, which effectively illustrates the despair he felt and the difficulty he faced in completing his film.

He eventually did complete his documentary, and Marlene was thoroughly displeased at the result. She insisted her voice had been dubbed. She did not recognize the slurring drunken speech as her own, neither the German nor the English, both of which were barely lucid, often rambling, and certainly incoherent. She demanded the film be re-edited, or better still, destroyed.

But Schell's work had resulted in an intriguing film about Dietrich the star and recluse. There were moments of sadness. "Bitter in childhood, sweet in adolescence, tragic in old age," she had once said. No current picture of her was allowed to be presented in Schell's film, but the camera showed the worn-at-the-edges, threadbare state of the Paris apartment, which was both prison and refuge to her, as well as glamorous stills from her amazing career.

The fact she didn't appear in the film makes the viewer long to see her, and one is kept in a state of anxious anticipation, hoping for a glimpse of Dietrich, once a legend, now a phantom. But she is never seen in person during the entire length of the documentary.

The film was shown at festivals, and soon mounting murmurs began to circulate about this odd, contrary, fascinating documentary. It won many awards at various international film festivals and was eventually nominated for an Academy Award, but lost to the excellent *The Times of Harvey Milk.* It was a hard choice for Academy voters, especially gay ones, torn between the choice of two gay icons. Milk over Marlene!

Secretly pleased at its reception and convinced her legend was still potent (as indeed it was), Dietrich withdrew her disapproval of the film and despite her previous statements, declaring the film was "ghoulish" and "grave-robbing," she approved the outcome.

A whole slew of books about Dietrich's life were published over her lifetime, recording her influence, the control with which she managed her image, her movies, and her love affairs. There were coffee table books with photographs of her in costume for her various films and concerts, photographs with her many lovers, photographs of her without her many lovers. But with her death in 1992 came a virtual waterfall of books about Dietrich.

A publishing phenomenon!

And so the legends, myths, might-have-beens still

keep turning up. To this day there is rarely a biography of an actor working in the thirties, forties, fifties, or sixties where Dietrich is not mentioned in the index. The same is true of Coward.

They were everywhere. They knew everyone. Which, I suppose, is the reason they continue to fascinate the world so many years later.

CHAPTER TWENTY-ONE

Les Avants (The Wrong House)

Eduardo and I decided to visit Switzerland, where Coward had bought and maintained a much bigger home than his Jamaican hideaway. After his death his heir Graham Payn occupied it. On the way back from this adventure, we planned a pilgrimage to Paris. We intended to stand outside Dietrich's apartment, hoping we would observe her peeking through the curtains.

A vague, unthought-out plan, and it was the first time I had arranged a visit to both my "parents" on the same trip.

From Paris we went to Geneva by bullet train, hurtling from France into Switzerland, the countryside a blur, finally reaching Geneva, a prim city with lots of chocolate, five-star hotels, cuckoo clocks, and a plethora of banks.

We stayed overnight in one of the five-star hotels, Le Richemond, and the next day hired a car and driver to take us to Les Avants, the tiny town in which Coward had lived. In spite of the ambition of our plans, I had failed to note something as simple as his address. As usual, my homework was shoddy and lazy, so the only reference I had to go by was Dame Rebecca West's description of the house as "opposite Dame Joan Sutherland's chalet" and "looking like a boarding school."

Our driver knew Les Avants but did not know of Coward, nor had he heard of Joan Sutherland. Her house, we knew, was called Chalet Monet. The driver had heard of that.

Les Avants consists of few scattered homes in the hills above Montreux, an out-of-fashion summer resort on the banks of Lake Geneva. It is dominated by a finishing school for girls, with a small all-purpose grocer's shop where one can order coffee and a croissant and have breakfast on wobbly chairs at wobbly tables.

Les Avants is reached by cable car from Montreux. It has a sleepy and unhurried charm.

I identified Sutherland's home by its plaque on a wall stating that it was in fact Chalet Monet. Across the road, opposite it, was a small house without any apparent distinction, architectural or otherwise. But since it was "opposite Dame Joan's," as Dame Rebecca West had declared, I presumed it to be Coward's house. Obviously he liked small houses since Firefly was also small. Still, I could not imagine guests of the caliber Coward entertained being very comfortable in this Les Avants home.

Nor did I understand West's boarding house reference, but she could be quite opaque at times in her writing.

The house had no privacy of any kind—no garden, no pool, no charm. Vivien Leigh's luggage alone would barely fit, and how could ladies of the elegance and style of Margaret Leighton, Lilli Palmer, and Irene Worth not turn around and return to Montreux where at least there was a grand, if slightly Miss Havisham-like, hotel?

We approached the house. No one seemed to be at home so I thought it safe to take some souvenir pictures. I stood at the door, at the window, in the path approaching the main door, I was photographed at all of these points, along with pictures taken looking east west north and south—my hand on my heart, a smile on my face. Although I had grave doubts that I was at the right house, I didn't want to admit this to Eduardo.

Deeply disappointed by the smallness and suburban quality of the house, but refusing to show any emotion other than pleasure at being there, I returned to Geneva with Eduardo and set off on a trip that was meant to take us to Gstaad, Lucerne, Zermatt, St. Moritz, and finally Zurich, but I called a halt to these plans in Gstaad, as I became claustrophobic in these heavily mountained surroundings. I couldn't stand it anymore.

"The mountains spoil the view," I told Eduardo.

"The mountains *are* the view," he responded.

"I can't stand them. They hem me in," I replied. "We will return to Paris tomorrow."

Eduardo was exasperated. "We still haven't seen Lucerne or..." his voice trailed off. I could sense his disappointment. I felt foolish. I was convinced that we hadn't seen Coward's house, but out of shame did not share this with Eduardo. I was angry with myself for not asking someone in Les Avants where Coward's house was. Sheer stubborn pride on my part.

"We are going back to Paris," I said, ending any further discussion.

Concierges and timetables were consulted, and then back on the bullet train, racing through the same blur of countryside, through Switzerland and France. We traveled in silence, avoiding the glances at one another.

Eduardo didn't like me that day. The mountains had got in the way.

CHAPTER TWENTY-TWO

Fireworks in Paris

It was July 14, Bastille Day, and there we were back in Paris.

We strode up and down Avenue Montaigne looking up at the fourth floor windows of number 12, where Dietrich lived in exile, attended to by two servants and hosting frequent visits from her daughter, Maria Riva, who lived in America.

According to reports, the servants and her daughter were the only people Dietrich saw. A dear friend and admirer of Dietrich, the German actress/singer Hildegard Knef, had tried phoning many times only to have the voice on the phone (which Knef knew was Marlene's) say, "Madame is in Japan" and then hastily hang up.

Like us, Knef used to stand on the opposite side of the Avenue, outside the grand hotel Plaza Athenee, where we had booked a room. From sidewalk or hotel room we could watch for movement from Dietrich's apartment. However, neither Knef nor Eduardo nor I ever saw any movement, so one can only guess what went on behind closed curtains.

According to first-hand accounts, Dietrich was abed, often drunk, testy, difficult, demanding, her beautiful legs swollen. She said she had been "photographed to death." No more cameras, no more visitors, the phone her only contact with the outside world, her friends diminishing by the day as death claimed them. "The wall of death" in her apartment continuously growing, almost no room left. She hung the photographs of deceased friends with an air of triumph. She had outlasted them.

She would control her last years as she had her glory years—no photographic record of her aging would ever be allowed.

The Avenue Montaigne was a highly suitable street for Dietrich to live on, as she would until she died there in 1992. Between the Champs Elysées and the Seine River banks, in the so-called "golden triangle," the wide street is home to the fanciest fashion houses in Paris. Her neighbors were Ungaro, Dior, Nina Ricci, Chanel, Chloe, as well as jeweler Bulgari, luggage maker Louis Vuitton, and it was home, too, to the Theatre des Champs Elysées, where in November 1948 Coward had performed in French the most autobiographical of his plays, *Present Laughter*, translated by Andre Roussin and retitled *Joyeaux Chagrin.*

Eduardo and I chose to eat at the renowned Maison Blanche, immediately opposite Dietrich's apartment house.

At the conclusion of the meal, all diners were asked to join the owner and staff on the roof of the restaurant. With wine glasses in our hands, we were invited to take our seats in one of the rows of beautifully upholstered chairs set out. And there for forty-five minutes, a display of fireworks shooting high, bursting into chrysanthemums, dervish-whirls, soaring, dipping, curtains of rockets, fountains of fire sweeping across the sky, a carnival of color and noise – a spectacle that Ziegfeld would envy. The symbol of Paris—the Eiffel Tower—stood proudly in golden witness to this grand display.

Of course, this brilliant display was for the national holiday Bastille Day, but I liked to think it was tribute to Dietrich—a graceful thank you from the nation of

France for her continued presence in their beloved, beautiful capital. Until her death, the brightest of all the brilliant crown jewels of the Avenue Montaigne.

I hoped she could see it all from her apartment.

CHAPTER TWENTY-THREE

Soundtrack of Two Lives

In 1973, ten years before I met Eduardo, when I was still working at Hurok Concerts in New York, I had an intense and passionate love affair with an artist named Robert Hoppe. We parted and for a time lost touch.

Shortly after Eduardo and I returned from Paris, Robert Hoppe re-entered my life.

We had met through mutual friends at a dinner party on Fire Island and discovered a shared interest in the music of the twenties and thirties. Gershwin, Porter, Kern, and Coward were the soundtracks of our lives: indeed, even more esoteric composers such as Robert Stolz, Noel Gay, and Vivian Ellis featured in our repertoire.

Hoppe (as I knew him—others called him Robert) was an artist who painted great Ziegfeld-like canvases, with dozens of chorus girls and boys, endless staircases, and curtains that draped and hung, were either rising or falling or billowing amid the choreographed movement of his dancers.

We first met as weekend guests at a Fire Island house and experienced an instant attraction across a dining table. Everyone else in the room disappeared into a murky background as Hoppe and I talked of the little-known artists we both celebrated and no one else present knew or showed any interest in. We kept bringing names into the conversation that we thought would stump one another, but none did.

This conversation led to his next painting. It

featured our favorite people whose celebrity had faded over the years, and thus the painting was titled "Forgotten Follies."

Neither Coward nor Dietrich was part of this work, as they were not forgotten. But there was Dorothy Dickson, Robert Ross ("friend of friends" as Oscar Wilde referred to him), Noel Gay, Evelyn Laye, the great Ziegfeld showgirl Dolores, and others not of the theater, but remarkable for one distinction or another: Norton the First, self-proclaimed Emperor of America and Protector of Mexico, writer Denton Welch, Sir Richard Burton (the explorer), and Isabelle Eberhardt (the only woman known to drown in a desert).

One group of people featured in this painting (which I now proudly own) were approaching the "stage" from a sunken staircase, while others descended from the top of the staircase towards "the stage," causing a major collision if they were to meet. However, this act was avoided, as they were all to be hidden by a massive curtain descending over the lot of them.

It was obviously inspired by the "Pretty Girl is Like a Melody" number from *The Great Ziegfeld*, which alternated with *Gone With the Wind* as Hoppe's favorite movie.

After dinner that night, Hoppe and I volunteered to clear the table and load the dishwasher since no one was interested in us and our esoteric conversation.

"Do you know who my favorite operetta composer is?" Hoppe asked, a touch of worry in his voice that seemed to imply that if I didn't know his favorite composer we couldn't be friends.

"Who?" I asked, hoping I knew.

Hoppe was hesitant. "I...I...I..." He couldn't bring himself to tell me.

"Come on, Hoppe, tell me."

It came out in a rush.

114

"I...I ...Ivor Novello." There, it was said, out in the open.

Of course I knew Ivor Novello. I began to sing. "We'll gather lilacs in the spring again..."

Hoppe's eyes bulged, and he dropped and broke a dish.

At the time of our meeting, the music of the world was of James Taylor, Joan Baez, Joni Mitchell, Judy Collins, Patti Smith, and Eric Clapton—not one of whose songs either of us knew. But Ivor Novello, Edward German, and Franz Lehar—these we knew and revered. And so a deep and lasting friendship was born over a broken plate on Fire Island and the composer Ivor Novello, a contemporary and rival of Noël Coward, made his way into the "Forgotten Follies" painting.

Novello's shows, which occupied the vast Theatre Royal Drury Lane in London from the mid-thirties until the end of World War II, all had titles that suggested names of perfumes at a Bloomingdale's counter: *Glamorous Nights, Crest of the Wave, The Dancing Years King's Rhapsody,* and *Perchance to Dream,* the latter the source of "We'll Gather Lilacs," Novello's last show was entitled *Gay's the Word.* Fitting? Ironic? We didn't care.

To be truthful, Novello's music was perfumed, too. Strings and harps and waltzes, swirling costumes, titled characters from Ruritania, handsome highwaymen, and kings putting duty before love are the hallmarks of his plays. And because Novello was the leading man in all of them, yet had no singing voice, the scores were written for female voices—duets between sopranos and contraltos. There was generally one tenor solo, sung by a minor character, and Ivor himself would speak the lyrics to a song that a female would complete in soaring fashion.

The stories and scores were old-fashioned stuff

much beloved by English audiences who fell in love with its unsophisticated and unashamedly romantic kitsch. As for American audiences, Novello as actor/writer/composer never made the journey across the Atlantic successfully.

Much to our delight, Hoppe and I discovered our apartments in New York City were one block apart, and at least once a week we had what we called "big fat nights" where we played music for one another in the hope we would surprise each other with a melody unknown to one of us. We would sit on the floor, choosing a record from a mountain of long-playing records.

"Do you know this one?" one of us would ask.

"What about this?" the other would interject.

Other men our age would be out at the gym or the bar or flirting with girls (or boys), while we sat on the floor of one another's apartment, introducing each other to heart-clutching, eye-rolling music.

These evenings would end late, the sky turning pink with the arrival of dawn, and we would go to bed and make love to each other, the music swirling around us. Wagner's *Rienzi* overture became a favorite for this exercise.

Hoppe's most-loved operetta was Jerome Kern's *Show Boat;* mine of course, Coward's *Bitter Sweet.*

After five short years of glorious companionship and weekly big fat nights, we drifted apart, the affair ending in 1978. Nevertheless, we remained great, loving friends.

Then in 1986, Hoppe was diagnosed with AIDS and he re-entered my life. He had moved to Los Angeles to stay with his sister. Eduardo and I had already moved from New York and so I was living in Los Angeles myself.

He was one of the early victims of the AIDS

plague and the treatments proved as toxic as the disease. Protocol of the time demanded treatment with a substance called AZT, now out of use, too poisonous for the body to sustain.

Also noticeable in the first wave of AIDS patients was the appearance of Kaposi's sarcoma; large, unsightly purple patches that popped up on the skin. Up until the outbreak of this disease, Kaposi's had been limited to elderly Jewish gentleman. Today it seems to have disappeared totally from people with AIDS.

Hoppe's legs were splattered by these bruised rash-like markings.

We resumed our big fat nights—Andrew Lloyd Webber's sweeping scores entering our consciousness and causing great excitement and delight. The discovery of singers such as David Knight, Sally Ann Howes, David Carroll, Zarah Leander, Karen Akers, Anne Zeigler, and Webster Booth. Oh, so many fed our souls!

Towards the end of his life, I would spend a great part of each week with Hoppe, for who else was there who shared such music obsessions and eccentric references?

One day we were at a restaurant where we were seated against a mirrored wall; the talk was whether Peggy Wood was better than Evelyn Laye as the leading lady of *Bitter Sweet* (one played it in London, the other in New York) and have there ever been singers to equal Helen Morgan or Gertrude Lawrence?

Suddenly the sun hit the mirror of the restaurant, and Hoppe turned and saw his reflection.

"We are leaving!" he announced abruptly and did just that, while I stayed behind to settle the bill.

I joined him outside the restaurant where he was trembling and in obvious distress. "What is it?" I implored.

"When the sun hit that mirror"—a gesture to the

restaurant's wall—"I could see splotches of Kaposi's under the makeup." (He used pancake to hide the unforgiving Kaposi marks.)

"Please take me home," he begged.

He never left his sister's home again, except for frequent stays in the hospital and trips to his doctor.

"I have CM," he told me one day, as tubes fed him, wires recorded his heartbeat, and machines showed his steady decline.

"Carmen Miranda?" I asked brightly.

"Charles Manson," he shot back.

We laughed. We could always find laughter or music to lessen the pain – and we tried to ignore and rarely spoke about the inevitable end.

He slept a lot, his head to one side on the pillow. I would hold his hand and sing—well, attempt to sing—"I'll See You Again."

After these visits, he never ever said goodbye to me. "See you," he would say instead. "I will know when to say goodbye," he once told me, with a smile.

The remark, so final, sent a chill through me.

The New Sadler's Wells Opera Company announced they would be presenting a production of Coward's *Bitter Sweet* at London's Coliseum Theater in early 1988.

At the time I was working on my first ever TV series, *The Wonder Years*, and it would be possible for me to leave Los Angeles on a Friday evening flight, arrive in London in time to be taken to the Coliseum, see the production, stay overnight at an airport hotel, and be back in Los Angeles in time for Monday morning's work.

It seemed a daunting exercise. I was afraid of the flight being delayed, arriving in London late, and missing the play (after all it was eleven hours in the air).

I timed the adventure as though it were a bank

heist. If the plane were three hours late, I would miss *Bitter Sweet.* This horrible fate kept me awake at night. I tossed, I turned, I read and re-read the glowing notices from London, all spilling and spinning with superlatives. The *Sunday Express* said, "The whole show beautifully mounted (by Ian Judge) is so spotless and well mannered that I hardly dare clear my throat for fear of breaking the magic spell," and The *Sunday Times* swore, "Generous-hearted is what this charming dated mixture is. It would be all too easy to mock. But instead, it is played straight and sincere, unafraid of pathos—and the gamble pays off. The production renders perfectly the sad, restless mood of the piece: that of eternal twilight."

I debated the logistics. To go or not to go? That became a question that tumbled around in my mind for a couple of weeks. I felt like Cybulski.

I was driving myself mad, Eduardo, too as well as my travel agent who kept booking and canceling flights. Hoppe, from his sickbed, kept urging me to go.

"If only you could come with me," I sighed.

"Well, I can't and that's that!"

Eventually, finally, I decided no, I would not go. I comforted myself with the thought that if the New Sadler's Wells Opera Company was mounting a first class production of the operetta that received such brilliant reviews, other opera companies would inevitably follow suit. I was sure New York City Opera would produce it, and I could go to it easily enough from Los Angeles, without the cliff-hanging fears of not making it in time. But as far as I could tell—with daily references to the Noël Coward Society website—no other company in the world—not even South Africa, Chad, or Lichtenstein—was about to present the operetta.

Hoppe and I did see the definitive production of *Show Boat* produced and directed lavishly by Harold

Prince on Broadway a few seasons earlier. A recording of the Kern show had been made with major talents Frederica von Staade, Teresa Stratas, and Jerry Hadley, including numbers cut from the original production and never heard by Hoppe until the release of the two- disc recording.

The *Show Boat* recording became the soundtrack of the last year of Hoppe's life. We had copies of it near his bed so that he could listen to it whenever he wanted. I had a copy in my car, so that on trips to the doctor and hospitals he could hear it, and I had a copy at my home, just in case he ever came to visit.

That score gave him immeasurable pleasure; he had a habit of closing his eyes and clutching his heart when he was moved by music. It was not an affectation at all but a simple, natural, authentic reaction.

When he would open his eyes and he saw me nearby, he smiled. Sometimes a huge grin, sometimes just a slight upward movement of his lips. Tears would trickle from his eyes. It could have been the music or it could have been death staring him in the face. Whatever the reason, I was always pleased to see the smile, and we would squeeze one another's hands.

I never tired of the Kern score, which I must have heard at least a hundred times in the last year of Hoppe's life. I have not listened to it since. I don't think I could.

Hoppe's health was deteriorating. We talked of frivolous things and sometimes of weighty things. He became convinced that there was an afterlife.

"What do you imagine it will be like?" I asked.

"Perfection," he replied. "A Ziegfeld number. I will be in top hat and tails. I will have a cane, and I will be leading a group of a thousand chorus boys down the most glorious set of stairs ever created."

Well, it gave him pleasure to think about it and it got him through the night. But privately I felt an eternity spent doing this would soon become rather tiresome. However, I kept this thought to myself.

I told my friend, the choreographer Agnes de Mille, of Hoppe's belief that the afterlife would be "perfection."

"Oh, I do hope not," she cried. "The struggle! The struggle is everything!"

After a day of watching Hoppe's restlessness, pain, and worry, I began to will him to die, for there was not much left for him. The soundtrack of *Show Boat*, chips of ice rubbed on his lips, and constant changes of T-shirts (which became drenched in day and night sweats) were the main events of his day.

"Do you want to go?" I whispered to him as I slipped a dry T-shirt over his head.

"Not yet," he answered. "I am still negotiating with God."

I saw him the day he died. His family and his closest friends were gathered around the pool of his sister's beautiful Mediterranean-style house in Toluca Lake, an upscale community in the San Fernando Valley. Talk was sporadic, meaningless. Just words for the sake of sound. It was one of those Californian days where people say, "Isn't this weather just perfect?" Perfect weather for the death of my best friend.

We went in, one by one, to sit with him. It reminded me of childhood visits to my mother's bedroom. This once beautiful man, god-like and golden, was now bloated, splotched, lying without movement, in and out of consciousness. I took his hand.

"It's Michael," I said, not sure if he knew who I was or who anyone else was, for that matter.

"I know," he murmured.

"I love you," I said

"I love you, too. Always have," he answered

"Do you want me to stay awhile?" I asked. "We

needn't talk."

"No," came the reply. "It's easier alone."

I bent down and kissed his furnace-hot forehead.

"Goodbye," he said.

I remembered him telling me he would know when it was time to say goodbye. Now, it appeared, was the time. I knew that I would never see him again. Nor would anyone ever share to the same degree the glories of "our" music, "our" world of forgotten follies.

I left his room, shaking.

At midnight my phone rang. It was Hoppe's sister. The two of us had bonded tightly over his deathbed; we had shared last moments, long conversations, changed his clothes, bathed him, emptied his chamber pot.

"It's happened," she cried. "Robert died at eleven thirty tonight."

"Thank you for letting me know, darling."

But I already knew.

I walked outside—it was a "perfect" night following a "perfect" day.

A hunter's moon strode across the cloudless sky on its nightly journey, suddenly disappearing behind trees then revealing itself as it came through on the other side of the trees. A hide and seek moon.

I let out a primal scream. It began in my toes and traveled up my body and out of my mouth into the night air. I rocked back and forth. I was keening.

The next day I got in my car and drove without direction. Up hills, down hills, around corners. I found myself at Tower Records on Sunset Boulevard. This was where Hoppe and I had bought his three copies of *Show Boat*, and where we spent many happy hours searching through bins for treasures.

I don't know what compelled me to go into the store, but I did and made my way to Original Cast Recordings. The New Sadler's Wells Opera two-disc recording of *Bitter Sweet* jumped out at me. Valerie Masterson, Martin Smith, and Rosemary Ashe were the stars. I bought two copies—one for me, one for Hoppe.

"*How silly,*" I thought. But if I lost one or wore one out, I had another. Hoppe's copy.

I opened my purchase in the car. Photographs of the principals, an account of how Coward came to write the piece, the story of the operetta that accompanied the discs.

I put the CD in the car player and made my way up Sunset Plaza Drive, a winding uphill ribbon of a road from the crest of which a magnificent view of the city of Los Angeles, from the Pacific Ocean to the San Bernardino Mountains, was laid out.

The overture to *Bitter Sweet* (which I had never heard, as the full score had never been recorded) begins faintly with a solo piano almost like Palm Court afternoon tea music. Then an oboe soulfully joins in—a flurry of violins—the piano again—and then with ravishing, startling strength, the entire orchestra, then finally the chorus joining in with a song I had never heard, "Play Something Romantic." It was one of the songs I would have brought to Hoppe as a "special find"—one we would have listened to, eyes rolling, clutching hearts together in a world that only existed between the two of us.

I parked the car, my vision too blurry with the beginning of tears to navigate the bends of Sunset Plaza Drive.

I remained there for the entire score. The melody "I'll See You Again" (my all time favorite) came very early in the work, and I could no longer hold back the tears, the gut wrenching tears. I wept like Medea. I wept for all the children who died before their lives began. I wept for all the wives who became widows during wars. I wept for all my friends—over a hundred—who had died from the plague of AIDS, which was raging then at its peak, I wept until there were no tears left in me, until no more sobs could be wrenched from me.

When the score had completed its ascending melodies, its sweet, old-fashioned Valentine card songs, its lonely sighs, I drove on.

I had been parked on the side of a road, safely around a turn. The number of the house opposite where I had parked was 1573 Sunset Plaza Drive. It looked to be modest home, but later when I was house-hunting I had occasion to enter it. Built on a mountainside it was terraced with large well-appointed rooms, more French windows than you could count, and an Olympic-sized swimming pool. A place fit for a star. I learned that it was this house that Noël Coward had rented when M-G-M was making their film of *Bitter Sweet*

An irony itself, which was bitter sweet.

CHAPTER TWENTY-FOUR
Les Avants (The Right House)

When Eduardo and I returned home after the abortive trip to the wrong house in Les Avants, I consulted my books on Coward—something I should have done in the first place—and saw on closer examination that he lived next door to Dame Joan Sutherland, which I guess can be called "opposite," not across the road as I had assumed.

A second trip was required.

This time Eduardo and I stayed at the Beau Rivage Hotel in Geneva. The manager showed us to the "Sissi Suite," so named for Elisabeth, Empress of Austria and Queen of Hungary, a fiercely independent woman who is still remembered fondly in Austria—particularly Vienna in much the manner Diana, Princess of Wales is remembered in England.

Sissi had left the hotel in 1898 at the height of the Hapsburg dynasty, of which she was a remarkable and impressive presence. She was accompanied by her lady-in-waiting with the intention of boarding a steamer to take her to Montreux. Before boarding the boat, she was suddenly attacked and stabbed by a demented anti-royalist Italian. He had intended to kill the Prince of Orleans, but as he later said, "Any royal would do."

Heavily corseted, the Empress Elisabeth did not realize she had been stabbed until she was on the steamer, where she felt faint, collapsed, and died in the arms of her lady-in-waiting. The death of a beloved Hapsburg—very much the stuff of operetta and melodrama, surely a life that Coward had read about.

We took a train rather than the steamer to Montreux, and after lunching at the Hotel Excelsior, we boarded a funicular cable car to Les Avants. We walked up the hill past the familiar store, past the girl's finishing school to Rue de Sunloup on which Coward's home stood. "Chalet Coward," known locally as Chalet Covair. I had done my homework this time!

Coward's chalet was next to Sutherland's and in the same alpine style. Quite large and totally suitable for a man of his accomplishments.

There were three cars parked in the graveled driveway. No forbidding gates, wide-open for visitors, so we walked to the front door and knocked at least three times and waited for a period of at least three minutes for it to be answered.

It appeared that there was no one there.

I later learned from Graham Payn's memoir, *My Life With Coward,* that it was not uncommon for "fans" to come unbidden to the house and ask for entry. Such unwelcome unannounced visits particularly vexed Payn quite understandably and he would play possum until they left.

Believing the house to be unoccupied despite the cars, we explored the grounds: once again I posed for photographs, clutching my heart and smiling insanely with delight as Eduardo recorded our visit.

At last I saw what Dame Rebecca West meant with her boarding house reference. Three stories with balconies, where swimsuits could be hung to dry, every window commanding a view of the village immediately below and the town of Montreux even further below, looking like a painted theater set. Still further was the sea, and on the other side of the water, France.

It was Coward's favorite residence, and the famous came as guests: the David Nivens, the Charlie Chaplins, the Ian Flemings, old lifelong friends like Joyce Carey and Judy Campbell, and of course Marlene Dietrich.

I walked onto the lawn, where high hedges shielded the view from the road. It was here that beach chairs had been set out with little tables for afternoon drinks. I could hear music from Dame Joan's house, carried by the breeze.

Call it a strong sense of birthright entitlement, but I felt no sense of intrusion as I mounted the steps of my "father's" home leading to a wooden deck, where I peered through the big windows into the living room. There was no doubt this was Coward's home.

A sculpture he had owned since the mid-thirties was placed over the fireplace at one end of the room. It consisted of two large angel wings with a clock in the middle and fantastically named "Tempis Fuget." There is an iconic photograph of The Master sitting in a chair with the sculpture behind him, the clock invisible, blocked by Coward as he poses regally in a chair. The end result is a photograph looking as though the wings are coming from his shoulders. Saint Noël.

At the other end of the room was a grand piano, its top crowded with photographs of the famous, inscribed to him with love: Maria Callas, Rudolf Nureyev, Ina Claire, Gertrude Lawrence, Marlene Dietrich, Vivien Leigh, Greta Garbo, David Niven, Sir Laurence Olivier—a veritable who's who of the international celebrities of his day. They were less than twelve feet from me, and I could see them quite clearly.

On the wall behind the piano was a portrait of Coward by Graham Sutherland.

The rest of the room, like his Jamaican home, looked cozy and comfortable, sofas and chairs one could sink into, coffee tables laden with newspapers and magazines and books, a home where one could, without fear, chuck off one's shoes and put stockinged feet up on the furniture.

I imagined the laughter, the music, the air of love that must have filled that room. The place Vivien Leigh came for comfort when her marriage to the love of her life, Laurence Olivier, dissolved. This was where Coward rehearsed actresses Lilli Palmer and Irene Worth for his *Suite in Three Keys,* the last play he appeared in London's West End. Illness prevented him from repeating the program of the three plays in New York, all set in the same suite of a hotel in Geneva. It was posthumously performed on Broadway with Hume Cronyn playing the roles Coward had written for himself. Jessica Tandy and Anne Baxter replaced Lilli Palmer and Irene Worth. It was renamed *Noël Coward in Two Keys* for its Broadway incarnation (this was the production Eduardo had seen).

Although I could see into only one room, I stood there, a stranger/intruder at the window for what seemed like hours. (Eduardo told me it later it was nearer fifteen minutes.) I imprinted the images in my mind like a camera recording the scene. I wanted to remember every detail of this moment always.

Of course, I had seen photographs of the room when it had been peopled. Dietrich had sat on the chintz-covered sofa with multiple cushions, her shoes off, feeling safe among her peers. Here in Les Avants, a faraway place, they could congregate, forget the legends and myths they so zealously created for themselves, controlling every public moment. They could be "normal." They could be silly. They could be themselves.

Whoever was in the house at the time of our visit, if in fact anyone was there at all, hid themselves from my view. Still, I felt welcome even though I'm sure I was not.

Eduardo told me he had never seen me as joyous as

I was that afternoon.

And I cannot remember another occasion when I was so full of joy.

CHAPTER TWENTY-FIVE

Dietrich's Death

Marlene Dietrich died in Paris of renal failure on May 6, 1992. She was ninety years old. On that day, Eduardo and I were working in Portland, Oregon, on a long-forgotten movie, *Body of Evidence,* starring pop singer/actress Madonna, who had recently released a music video paying homage to movie goddesses, including Marlene. I was not unmindful of the coincidence. Dietrich had outlived most of her lovers and most of her friends. She died in her sleep, lulled by alcohol and pills and presumably her Fernando Lamases.

Her last film appearance, in 1978, was negotiated by daughter Maria Riva. It was a miserable and humiliating experience for Marlene and a forgettable film, *Just a Gigolo,* starring David Bowie and directed by David Hemmings.

Her participation called for two days work in Paris, despite the fact that the major portion of the movie was shot in Germany. A set for Marlene's scene was built in Paris. It was, mercifully, a brief scene. She sang the title song, wearing a most unflattering costume: no flesh showing as in the old days, a wide-brimmed hat with a spider's web veil that made her look more like a caricature of Dietrich rather than the icon. Despite flowery billing that read "...and featuring, with great pride, MARLENE DIETRICH." She and the film were panned cruelly by reviewers.

From her bed, reviewing the stills from the movie, she scrawled across a picture of herself, "How ugly can you get?" and refused to be photographed ever again. She realized the mistake she had made by agreeing to be in Hemmings' film. The contrast of the unique, sultry glamour she had created throughout her life with the drag queen look of *Just a Gigolo* was hard for her to witness.

The money, $250,000, however, was welcome.

In 1979, she passed out in her Paris bedroom (by this time she was fully alcoholic) and on awakening could not get up from the floor where she had fallen. She was smuggled out of the building on a stretcher and carried uncomfortably down the building's back staircase, rather than in the elevator, so as to avoid the unkind eyes of fellow apartment dwellers, who might have notified the ghoulish tabloid press. She was taken to a hospital for X-rays. A hairline fracture from a fall above the hip joint was found and bed rest was prescribed. The fracture would heal itself within four weeks.

Like my mother in New Zealand, Dietrich embraced bed rest. It gave her a reason to remain in reclusion.

For the rest of her life—another thirteen years—Dietrich remained in her bedroom, her only connection to the outside world the telephone, which she used extravagantly and without concern for the time of day anywhere or the cost or length of the call. It was not uncommon for Los Angeles friends to be wakened at 3:00 A.M. by Dietrich calling from Paris (noon her time).

Her daughter Maria arranged the funeral: Marlene Dietrich's last spectacular curtain call. Her casket, draped in the tricolor flag of hospitable France before the altar of La Madeleine, drew crowds numbering in the thousands turning out to pay homage to this great celluloid queen.

Then, a change of flag: France's was replaced by the American flag, a reminder of her citizenship and the country where her legend was born and flourished. The casket containing the body so many worshipped was flown to Berlin, accompanied by her devoted daughter.

As the hearse weaved through the now unified city of Berlin (the Wall had come down three years earlier) hundreds of Berliners threw flowers at the coffin.

Dietrich was taken to the small cemetery of Schoenberg, the suburb of Berlin where she had grown up and was now to be buried close to her mother.

Another change of flag to that of her native Germany before the coffin was laid to rest in the ground.

Her gravestone reads: *"Hier steh ich den Marken meiner Tage,"* translated by daughter Maria as, "Here I stand at the benchmark of my days," from a poem by the nineteenth-century writer Theodor Korner. However, Dietrich hoped, according to one biographer, it would be interpreted as, "I am what I am, I remain the proof of me."

Some years after Dietrich's death, Eduardo and I made a journey to the grave, with its neat little border of bricks and cover of flowers. It would have been a source of pride and consolation to Dietrich to know her final resting place was in the little cemetery, kept immaculately tidy and neat—a proper resting place for one as concerned for cleanliness as she was.

The day of our visit in autumn 1996, the graveyard was carpeted in damp, fallen leaves of gold and russet and brown. Eduardo and I said our goodbyes to her. In that moment I felt a closeness to her that I had never experienced. I was so grateful I had made this pilgrimage: a true moment of peace.

Standing before her grave, I realized now I was truly an orphan.

Eduardo was now my family.

CHAPTER TWENTY-SIX
Return to London

In 2003, Eduardo and I were hired to work on the movie *Sky Captain and the World of Tomorrow* to be shot at Elstree Studios in London. This was the studio where Dietrich filmed Hitchcock's *Stage Fright* over fifty years earlier. Hitchcock later referred to her as "the absolute professional: a professional wardrobe person, a professional director, and a professional lighting technician." It was a backhanded compliment at best, omitting to mention "a professional actress." Hitchcock, like Dietrich, had to control everything around him, always the center of the world.

However, realizing he was beaten, he abdicated his control when it came to Dietrich, who ordered a wardrobe from Dior, borrowed the song "La Vie en Rose" from her friend and one-time lover Edith Piaf, as well as commandeered Cole Porter's "Laziest Gal in Town," a song written in 1927 but which has become ever-identified with Marlene, who claimed it had been written for her. Also, according to reports from leading man Richard Todd, Dietrich directed the actors, as Hitchcock seemed disinterested in the film.

This would not apply to actress Jane Wyman, fresh off her Oscar-winning performance of a deaf mute in *Johnny Belinda.* Ms. Wyman was playing Dietrich's maid, a role she did not enjoy, and she was frightfully jealous of the glamour Dietrich was able to display, while Wyman was reduced to drab cardigans, even drabber dresses, and horror of horrors—flats!

133

Although not nominally the star of *Stage Fright,* Marlene received second billing to Jane Wyman. Dietrich's performance was the one all reviewer's crowed about. It remains (to this day) one of her best film performances.

So, as I walked through the gates of Elstree every morning, I imagined Dietrich, forever punctual, arriving in a chauffeured car for her complicated makeup, which included a complex set of tapes that "lifted" her face and were secured painfully to her scalp under a wig.

The movie Eduardo and I were working on at Elstree was the last movie (so far, anyway) that we were to make for producer Raffaella De Laurentiis, for whom we had now worked for over twenty years. We had an arrangement with her that we would never stay in the hotel that the rest of the crew was housed in. To keep costs down, she made "deals" with hotels such as Holiday Inn, Travelodge, Comfort Inn, and the like. Despite her economical reasoning, I had told her that if I died during production on one of her movies, I would hate my obituary to read, "He died in a Holiday Inn." For a child of Dietrich and Coward this would never do.

Through friends and hotel contacts I had arranged rooms for Eduardo and myself at the Savoy Hotel in London, at the same rate per night as the production was paying for the crew staying in lesser hotels. This was deemed a "favor" to me by the Savoy management and was not to be extended to the rest of the crew, who did not seem to mind at all. They liked the ambience the Moat Hotel at Elstree had to offer, particularly the bar.

However, the Savoy, mindful of their stature as a luxury hotel, extended the same rate to the high-caliber actors of our film, which included Angelina Jolie, Jude Law, Gwyneth Paltrow, Michael Gambon, Giovanni Ribisi, and most unexpectedly and sort of out-of-place, the "spacey" actress Bai Ling, who told me she was "born on the moon."

I believed her.

This is where Coward stayed when he had given up his residence in London, so once again I felt his echoes, followed his footsteps, and ate at his table in The Grill, as well as asking for a "Bullshot"—a drink he favored—consisting of vodka and beef bullion from the barman at the American Bar.

"No one has ordered a Bullshot since Sir Noël Coward was staying here," the bartender told me. He seemed mightily impressed at my request. I smiled nonchantly.

After a few sips, I discovered I did not like the drink at all and when no one was looking I poured it into a flower arrangement. (I think I heard a tulip scream.)

The situation of the Savoy Hotel, within walking distance of all West End theaters and a short hop, skip, and jump across Waterloo Bridge to the National Theatre, not only allowed but encouraged Eduardo and me to go to the theater almost every night.

Two Coward plays were seen back-to-back. The seldom-produced *Semi-Monde*, set in the bar at the Ritz Hotel in Paris, was produced at the Citizen's Theatre in Glasgow and brought into London because of its immense critical reception in Scotland. Cinematic in style, the attention moving easily from one group of people to another and the set done in black and white and gold, I was in heaven. It is near impossible to describe the plot, but it is the most representative of Coward's plays portraying the world of the rich and talented and famous in the twenties and thirties, more so than any other of his works.

Concerning itself with intrigue, clashes of the elegant guests of the Ritz, much martini drinking, cigarettes cases and lighters, secret affairs, and bitchy betrayals, *Semi-Monde* reaches its climax when one of the guests shoots his rival in love in the bar of Paris's Ritz Hotel.

Oddly enough, for a man who lived such a charmed life, Coward wrote very few happy endings. I don't think he believed in them. No serious dramatist does, when you come to think of it, for there are no happy endings in life.

Semi-Monde ends on a note where the characters have no one to blame but themselves for the emptiness and superficiality of their lives. Their suffering is of their own making.

A lesson to be learned: we are the architects of our own folly.

The many characters that people the play make it an expensive production to revive, and I felt extraordinarily grateful to be in London for its only West End production to this day. It became the twenty-third of the approximately forty plays and musicals Coward had written that I had seen. Over half of them!

I knew that it would be impossible for me to see the entire Coward canon, as many of the earlier plays were unsuccessful, and rightly so. They were exercises in which he was looking for his voice, which he would eventually find in *The Vortex* and create a body of work that would immeasurably enrich world theater and last forever. As the critic Kenneth Tynan wrote, "Coward was the Turkish bath in which English comedy slimmed."

As I left the performance of *Semi-Monde, I* said to myself, "Before I die, I must see a production of *Bitter Sweet*, the most successful and beautiful of Coward's operettas, and certainly my favorite of all his musical plays. My unwavering affection for it was based on recordings of the score. I had never seen a production of it however. It is seldom revived because of its size. It requires a mammoth cast, a large orchestra, and voices more suitable for opera than a musical. A major commitment for any company.

It became an ambition, a destination, a Holy Grail for me, much as Marco Polo made it his life's work to reach the Mongol Court. So I would search out a production of *Bitter Sweet,* wherever it could be found.

The same weekend we saw *Semi-Monde,* Eduardo and I were delighted by a revival of *Fallen Angels*, one of Coward's earliest plays, regularly revived and always successful. It was presented at the Apollo Theatre, next door to the Lyric where *Semi-Monde* was playing. An avenue of Coward!

Fallen Angels concerns two women who are best friends, now in middle age, awaiting the arrival of a Frenchman with whom they both had affairs in their youth. While waiting for him, they become tipsy and argumentative. They both claim they are the love of the Frenchman's life. Their exchange becomes accusative; the champagne is liberally poured and even more liberally consumed. They become incoherent, one accepting a cigarette from the other and when offered a match, refusing it. The unlit cigarette becomes a prop the actress does not know what to do with. She gesticulates with it, makes irrelevant points with it, "smokes" it before she eventually stubbornly stubs it out, still unlit.

Comedy arising out of character and situation—rather than jokes—pepper this slight play, which was perfectly acted at breakneck speed by Frances de la Tour and Felicity Kendall to an enraptured audience whose laughter filled the Apollo Theatre. Laughter was still occurring as the audience spilled into the street at the play's end. And as was the case with Eduardo and myself, the rest of the evening was punctuated by our own laughter as we recalled a piece of business, a sparkle of dialogue.

My visit to this play only made my desire to see *Bitter Sweet* even greater. Surely, a production of this operetta had to be mounted somewhere, sometime.

"Even if it is being performed by an all female cast in Dubai or Addis Ababa, we will go," I told a rather startled but pleasantly agreeable Eduardo.

CHAPTER TWENTY-SEVEN

A Dangerous Woman

One evening while still in London, still at the Savoy, still at Elstree Studios, still filming Sky *Captain and the World of Tomorrow*, yet another movie that would flop, we were drawn to a play with the titillating title of *A Dangerous Woman*. When we learned that the dangerous lady was Wallis Simpson, who became the Duchess of Windsor, we were more than intrigued. As devotees of the twenties and thirties and constantly on the outlook for echoes of these jazzy and troubled, rich and poor decades, we booked seats.

It was in what New Yorkers would call an off-Broadway theater: a small, well-decorated theater off Piccadilly Circus that one entered down a small, steep staircase.

A Dangerous Woman turned out to be virtually a one-woman show about the Duchess, wife of the exiled King of England who abdicated the throne for "the woman I love," as he so painfully said in his radio address to the nation.

In this play the recently widowed Duchess nervously awaits permission to be received at Buckingham Palace and attend the ceremonial funeral as the rightful wife of the former King. For the entire thirty-five years of her marriage to the Duke she had been denied access to the Palace and her royal relatives.

A Dangerous Woman was splendidly directed, all the notes of the play resounding like a virtuoso concert performance: waltz-like—one, two, three, fast, slow,

139

fast, one, two, three. Well-acted, nicely set, stylishly written, but the star of the production was the director, who had guided the play into a glittering and unexpected bubble of an evening.

The night was particularly memorable because the last line of the play had the audience group-gasp and then a sudden roar of laughter. Neither Eduardo nor I understood the laughter. The line made no sense to either of us. It did not seem funny and certainly did not warrant the uproarious and spontaneous response it received. We left a trifle baffled.

The reaction of the audience to the last line of the play kept niggling at me in the manner a sinus condition can bother the nerves of a tooth. I wrote to the euphoniously named Pip Pickering whom the program identified as the director. My letter was sent to him at the Jermyn Street Theatre on Savoy Hotel letterhead (to show I was serious), asking for an explanation of the laughter the play's last line.

Two days later the phone rang in my room at the Savoy. It was Pip Pickering.

I explained the difficulty I had with the end of the play, and he told me it was a local topical reference that no foreign visitor (such as Eduardo and I) would understand. It had something to do with England's first female Prime Minister, Dame Margaret Thatcher, and money. Anyway, even after Pip Pickering did his best to make it clear to me, it remained unclear, and I never understood why it caused such a cascade of laughter.

However, it did not matter, and to be polite, rather than thank him for calling me with this cloudy information and simply hanging up the phone, I asked Pickering what his future plans were.

"I want to direct all of Noël Coward's plays," he said with bright confidence.

My jaw dropped and the phone, too, slipping from

my grasp.

"All of his plays?" I asked, hoping I had not disconnected him.

I hadn't. "All of them," he repeated.

"Rat Trap and *This is a Man* and *Sirocco,* too?" I wondered aloud. These were early unsuccessful plays, which are even difficult to read today, let alone direct and sit through.

"All of them," he repeated with emphasis.

I had to meet this Pip Pickering.

"Could you join me and my friend for dinner next Tuesday?" I asked. "At the Axis," I added. The Axis is an Art Deco restaurant at the fashionable One Aldwych Hotel, near the Savoy. It had no connection with The Master at all. It hadn't been there in his lifetime, but I was sure that if he were still alive he would be a regular there, just as he was at the Ivy and the Savoy Grill.

Eduardo and I arrived first—as is our wont—and told the crisp maitre d' that we were expecting a friend, a Mr. Pickering.

The maitre d' made a note of this and showed us to a corner table. It was behind a screen such as actresses use to change costumes onstage or the one Lady Teazle hid behind in *A School for Scandal.* This screen prevented us seeing diners as they arrived at the restaurant, but it also afforded us great privacy.

We were much taken aback when the maitre d' announced, "Mr. Pickering has arrived," and instead of the plump, jolly, slightly disarrayed person we had imagined him to be, a tall, vibrant, well-dressed young man of twenty-two swept in.

Extending his hand he said, "I am the child of Elyot and Amanda." (These are the names of the lead characters in Coward's great play *Private Lives.*) I was amazed, astonished, delighted, enchanted, and totally riveted.

He was extremely elegant—thin as an exclamation mark, with long, dark, shiny black hair curling at the collar, pale-green eyes flecked with gold, and lashes that seemed to sweep the floor. His cheeks were apple-red like a schoolboy's ("As though they had just been slapped," he remarked when I complimented him on them.) He was androgynous and could easily model for Dolce & Gabbana or Tom Ford, who seemed to choose such male models for their clothing lines.

I heard an orchestra begin a Coward tune, although there was no orchestra present to play one. Throughout the dinner, I kept hearing a shuffle of Coward's songs. The restaurant became a setting for a play, and Eduardo and I became supporting actors to the non-stop dazzling performance by Pip Pickering.

He would pause every now and then, as if in a Pinter play, and just as I was about to add a thought or ask a question, he would start up again. He *was* a Pinter play. What he said, I cannot recall, but across the table, throughout the meal, I knew I had met someone quite extraordinary. I was prepared to drown in his eyes. He shared my 1920s and '30s view of life. His love of Coward began at age twelve when he read *Blithe Spirit* as part of a school project. It led him to explore the entire Coward canon, and he has remained a faithful devotee to this day.

Pip had insights into Coward that quite surprised me. "All Coward heroines are Noël himself," he told me, "and those nervous breakdowns he kept having throughout his life were symptoms of a bipolar disorder." *My goodness*, I thought, *feet of clay*, but it did not stop me from loving Coward. Nothing could. Nothing would. Pip and I were both Coward addicts. Neither of us had ever met such a kindred soul, not even Hoppe, who shared this obsession. It was exhilarating stuff for both of us.

Pip had no thoughts about Dietrich – he knew she figured in Coward's life and added that at one time Coward had attempted to write a musical for the two of them. This I never knew, so I sat rapt as Pip told me of it.

It had started out as a film script but as Coward wrote, it seemed more suitable as a musical. He gave it the working title of *Later Than Spring,* a tale of a widow and an exiled prince meeting at a grand hotel and falling in love. Coward even recorded some songs that he had written for them: for Dietrich there was "Family Dirge" and "Now I'm a Widow," for himself, "I Wanted to Show You Paris," and for them both in duet, the title song, "Later Than Spring."

This plan came to naught. Coward felt the characters were simply not coming alive for him. It was time to "sail away" and the musical, in fact, became *Sail Away*, which had no role for either of them, but featured the song *"Later Than Spring."* He made use of most of what he wrote as he did not like waste.

On the way back to the Savoy, I asked Eduardo what he thought of the evening.

"I felt like wallpaper," he answered.

"But such beautiful wallpaper," I replied.

This remark neither calmed nor pleased him.

For the rest of my stay in London, Pip Pickering would feature a great deal in my life, attending theaters with me, dining at Coward-like restaurants, drinks at the Rivoli Bar at the Ritz Hotel, a stream of talking, thoughts tumbling.

CHAPTER TWENTY-EIGHT
Bitter Sweet

Constant Internet checking on the Noël Coward Society website informed me of productions of *Blithe Spirit, Hay Fever, Private Lives, Present Laughter, Design for Living,* and *Fallen Angels* being mounted all over the world (royalty checks for the Coward estate must be flooding their offices). Suddenly, there was a mention of an amateur production of *Bitter Sweet* in Glasgow, Scotland.

I toyed with the idea of going to Glasgow for a while, but I ultimately decided against it. Amateurs? Scottish? *Aye, by God!* I thought to myself. The leading man as written is Austrian, and the entire second act of the play is set in Vienna. Glasgow and Vienna seemed a difficult, if not impossible, match.

But as weeks became months and months became years, I re-thought my decision. If I were to see *Bitter Sweet* before I died (it was the only thing left on my "bucket list"), I would go anywhere at anytime.

Coward wrote the lyrics, the music, and the book for *Bitter Sweet*. This is a singular achievement: very few musicals or operettas, or even operas for that matter, have the same creator guiding all aspects of the show. Even more impressive was the fact he did all of this at age twenty-eight. When produced in London, it was a major success at His Majesty's Theatre in the West End. Reviews sparkling with superlatives resulted in a stampede at the box office and a run of 761 performances.

The program proudly boasted: "The Entire Production by Noël Coward."

The New York presentation that followed was the last show the great Florenz Ziegfeld produced on Broadway. Once again Coward received notices that any artist would envy. The *New York Times* wrote, "The virtuosity of his talents amounts to genius." In the same review they designated it as "charming, subtle and witty." The New York run was cut short by the stock market crash of 1929, but achieved a moderate run of 159 performances.

Two films of the musical were made. The first, an English version starring Anna Neagle, omitted the third act of the play totally. The second, a Hollywood version made by M-G-M and featuring Jeanette MacDonald and Nelson Eddy, strayed far from the original and impertinently had "additional lyrics" by Gus Kahn. Coward summed up this film as "a rocking horse in love with a suitcase." He did not identify which of the stars he considered the rocking horse or the suitcase, but he never allowed a film of his work to be done again in Hollywood thereafter.

Almost as though I were being rewarded for my patience and determination, the Noël Coward Society website announced a production by the Light Opera Company of Chicago. My dream was about to come true. I was going to see a production of *Bitter Sweet* at last!

The Chicago production was everything I had hoped for and in fact more. The "more" being Eduardo's reaction.

I had told Eduardo little of the plot, and although he had heard the music played by me umpteen times, he does not like to listen to show music until after he has seen the play and knows the reason for the placing of the songs. Then it floods his domain.

He had embraced the song and lyrics of "If Love Were All" as his theme years ago, when he first heard the Pet Shop Boys recording of it, but never "got" "I'll See You Again" and why I wanted it be played at my memorial service. Optimism and mystery combined.

Now he thoroughly understands.

Bitter Sweet tells the story of a young woman, on the eve of her marriage, confiding in her friends that she is not in love with her fiancé but madly, insanely, truly in love with her music teacher. She is persuaded by a guest at the wedding party, an older, beautiful, and very distinguished woman named Lady Shayne, who many years ago was faced with the same dilemma, to take action. Not in romantic love with her betrothed but drawn irresistibly, irrevocably to her music tutor.

Lady Shayne (born Sarah Millick) tells her own story in flashback. She recounts how many years ago, she fled the stifling marriage arranged by her family and fled to Vienna with her piano teacher and how they became a singer/orchestra leader team in a Viennese café. Sarah—now Sari—is insulted by an Austrian officer. Her lover comes to her rescue and he is killed in a duel. Sari becomes an international prima donna and keeps alive the music her lover had composed.

The modern young woman who has listened raptly to Lady Shayne's story (as Sari is now known, having married Lord Shayne late in life) is so inspired by this romance, she decides to follow Lady Shayne's example. She flees the chains that bind her to an everyday life and runs away from her suffocating fiancé, family, and country to follow her dream. (A regular theme in Coward.)

Sentimental admittedly, but it is the sentiment of an old Valentine, reminding one of past loves, a pretty ache of memory as one goes through an old family album, or coming across ribboned love letters sent years ago. It has authenticity and truth, and unless you have a heart of stone it is impossible to avoid its message of true passion and an uncontrollable, all-consuming love, such as we all want and few of us ever experience.

So it was with high anticipation and vast expectations Eduardo and I entered the theater, an ivy-covered building, part of the Northwestern University campus in Evanston, twenty minutes from downtown Chicago. Six hundred seats, all filled, Eduardo on the aisle, two fashionable ladies to my right.

"Have you seen it before?" they asked. "No? Well, then you are in for a treat."

The stage was empty but for a grand piano.

My heart rushed as the lights dimmed. A young man in a tuxedo came onstage, sat at the piano, and he played the first chords of the operetta. He sounded just like the recording I'd bought of the New Sadler Wells production and listened to its score the day Hoppe died.

The music flowed, a curtain drew, revealing the orchestra onstage in a gazebo-like setting, and there we were at the eve-of-the-wedding party. Flappers and their bright, young tuxedoed men frozen in position, a Hoppe painting! The moment was still for a few seconds, only as the music changed from its romantic theme into a jazzy Charleston, the dancers came to life and a party was in full swing.

The orchestra remained onstage for the rest of the performance quite naturally, since the first and third acts take place at a London ball and the second at a Viennese cabaret (where they mysteriously spoke French rather than German). If there was a scene that did not require the orchestra (the piano lesson for instance or the specialty number "We All Wore a Green Carnation"), lights dimmed the musicians out and/or a curtain concealed them.

The leading performers were superb, the chemistry

between them almost tangible, so when the male lead died at the end of the second act, Sari is visibly, deeply heart-broken. And so are we.

It is never expected that the leading man would disappear from the play halfway through its course, but *Bitter Sweet* calls for just such an action. Sari's piano teacher/lover is killed in a duel at the end of Act Two, a gasp, a cry of surprise, and even a cry of pain came from the audience. A hush, broken only by a few tears as Sari rushes to his side and he dies in her arms.

The exchange between performers and audience was intense and electric. The silence of that moment was brilliant.

A sudden, almost jarring blackout, then intermission.

Eduardo and I were in tears as were many in the audience, the lobby full of sobs and the blowing of noses. Animated chatter anticipating the third act, which if it were as good as Acts One and Two would make it a performance no one present would ever forget, was heard all around.

In the third act Sari reprises the major song from the show, "I'll See You Again," as she finishes telling her story to the reluctant bride to be, remembering the passion and cruel death of her one true love in Vienna years ago.

There is a truth, a meaning, a depth to the song, the first flush of real love remembered in all its joyful intensity. It had for years been my favorite song. I still always have a recording of it nearby.

To Eduardo, it had been no more than a pretty melody. But seeing and hearing it in context touched him deeply. He understood what I had always known: that it is a song of true love, lasting affection, and real commitment. A song that celebrates love, even after death.

When planning our trip to Chicago to attend this production of *Bitter Sweet,* I did not consult Eduardo – I just told him we were going. I selfishly did not consider his reaction. This was a trip especially and totally for me.

At the first intermission, a sense of my self-absorption flooded me; I suddenly felt guilty for dragging him halfway across the country to see a show he had only limited interest in. I asked him diffidently, "Is it okay? Are you enjoying it?"

His eyes moist, he nodded and smiled the smile that has enchanted me for thirty years.

I fell in love with him all over again.

CHAPTER TWENTY-NINE
Dietrich Lives on in Berlin

Eduardo and I had last visited Berlin in 1996, when we made our pilgrimage to Dietrich's grave. Then it was a city of construction sites. A skyline of cranes. Jackhammers and traffic competing for decibel levels.

Thirteen years later in 2009 we planned a return trip. The Reichstag building had been rebuilt, the Holocaust Memorial unveiled, the Adlon Hotel re-opened. We visited all of these but the real reason for our visit was the Marlene Dietrich permanent exhibition at the new Film Museum, which had opened in September 2000. Her daughter, Maria, had gifted a lifetime of her mother's possessions to the museum: gowns, jewelry, shoes, hats, luggage (heavily initialed "MD" for easy recognition at airports, custom sheds and theaters), letters to and from lovers, as well as notes to herself. Two in particular, written in block letters, show anguish and tore at my heart: FRITZ LANG IS A SADIST INCORPORATED and the plaintive JOSEF VON STERNBERG IS MY MASTER – WHEN WILL HE RETURN?

There were also photos of every period of her life: as a young German actress struggling for recognition, a sudden bona fide German movie star with the release of the film *Blue Angel,* a huge star in America in the early thirties, in Army uniform entertaining the troops during the war, dressed in dazzling evening wear at Ciro's, Mocambo, Maxim's—everywhere deluxe. Alongside these personal photos were stills from her film appearances in the late forties and early fifties, when she reclaimed her movie eminence for a while and then lost it again. Photos of her emergence as a cabaret star – the famous nude dress, all of this and even more is recorded fully by the cameras: Marlene as "hausfrau," photos of her in kitchens preparing her famous *pot au feu*, with her grandchildren, with her daughter, with her husband and his longtime mistress. Pictures of her many lovers of both sexes: another testament to her strangled cries of being "photographed to death."

One photograph in particular grabbed my attention. It was the last photograph taken of her in Coward's company. In fact, it was the final public appearance by the now knighted Sir Noël Coward. It was the last time they saw each other, and the photographs of this occasion have a lovely, almost autumnal quality to them, their love and friendship for one another exquisitely and tenderly captured.

Another photograph caught my eye. It was shot at the 1950 Academy Awards ceremony held at Los Angeles's beautiful Pantages Theater before the event was internationally televised. Dietrich had never won an Oscar, but by sheer willpower she dominated the evening. I had known of the existence of this photograph for many years and was very much aware of the event at which it was taken, but I had never seen it in person before.

She had been invited to present what was then considered a minor award—Best Foreign Language Film—and the winner was *The Walls of Malapaga*. Most people do not remember the film; even fewer have heard of it, but everyone present that evening would always remember Marlene Dietrich.

Researching what the other women presenters and nominees – Marilyn Monroe, Helen Hayes and Debbie Reynolds among them—would be wearing (frilly, prom-like ball gowns), Dietrich chose a slinky black dress so form fitting it appeared to be painted on her. She had pre-determined which side of the stage to enter so that the knee-length slit in the dress would be revealed to full effect. The legs that had been called "the most beautiful in the world" were still worthy of that title. She strode on stage to a thunderous reception that became a standing ovation. As it turned out, this was the only standing ovation of the night.

She is photographed walking to the podium, the flash of her exquisite leg revealed at each step, a seductive half-smile playing across her features, sultry, sleepy eyes sweeping the house. She was in full control. Her plan to steal the evening thoroughly and brilliantly succeeded.

One entered the Berlin exhibit via a hallway that was entirely mirrored – floor, walls, and ceiling. It created an effect where the visitor was reflected a zillion times, his or her image coming together and breaking apart as if seen through a kaleidoscope. For a moment, you become Dietrich. You begin to understand how she must have felt when on public display: vulnerable yet proud. You understand the lifelong need she had to control her image as you view your own from every angle, automatically sucking in your stomach, correcting your posture—it is not easy to be Marlene Dietrich. The entrance to her exhibit was proof enough.

In spite of the times when Dietrich gave impromptu concerts to students and wartime concerts to soldiers, she never felt she was part of the crowd. She knew she was special, set apart. When asked to be interviewed by *People* magazine, she sniffed and said, "I am not people!" On another occasion at an airport, she looked around and said to her companion, "It is no wonder they pay me so much money. Look how ugly the public is!" These remarks were not meant to be funny. She was dead serious.

This museum has become the repository of her glory days. Film loops play, her songs linger in the air, even her secrets are revealed. On being photographed for instance: "The main spotlight was placed very low and far away from me. The secret face with the hollow cheeks was achieved as a result of placing the main spotlight close to my face and high above it." By holding her finger aloft and registering the heat, she knew when it was in the correct position.

Everything in her fifty-year career had been choreographed with care, every moment in public studied and rehearsed and eventually performed. She never checked her image in mirrors while out. She had done that before she left home (wherever that was). She knew how she looked at all times.

Because of the torrent of publicity Paramount Studios created for her, she was an American star before she was even seen in a movie in the United States. But the sensational impact she made in *Morocco* catapulted her to even greater fame. The suggestion of her bisexuality was acknowledged at a time when it was normally taboo and hidden. She did not care. She knew who she was. She dared. She provoked rebuke.

Apart from all the photos, I was hugely fascinated by the display of so many of her personal possessions. Here was the luggage which she "schlepped" everywhere along with her stage dresses, the daywear, the evening wear, also gifts from lovers—cigarette cases encrusted with jewels and inscriptions.

"I started smoking during the war," she once wrote. "I have kept it up ever since. It keeps me healthy." Years after this statement, while staying at Coward's chalet in Les Avants, he once said to her "Bet you can't stop smoking." "Of course I can," she answered and stubbed out her cigarette. She kept her word and never smoked again. "Proof of my stupidity," she announced.

Coward smoked to the end of his days. "He was right," she told the world. "His mother was dead, he had no children, and he was responsible only for himself, and therefore had the right to spend his years as he pleased."

To Dietrich people who give up smoking believe they will never die. "In reality," she said, "they die from other illnesses: intestinal cancer, stomach cancer, and cancer of the pancreas. To make cigarettes responsible for all this is a great injustice – why so much fuss over the way you die? Death is unavoidable."

Like most addicts of any kind, once she gave up cigarettes, she replaced it with another addiction: drink. She became alcoholic—a much uglier alternative, and it was wise of her to do it as a recluse.

Next to the display of her cigarette cases, in their way as beautiful as Faberge eggs, there was her passport, her military identification card, a musical saw, which became part of her act for the troops—she never played the saw to the paying public.

Continuing on our way through this extraordinary exhibition, Eduardo and I saw the clunky white telephone that sat by her bed and kept her in touch with the world after she had abandoned it, and next to the phone was her bulging telephone book whose clasp could barely keep it shut—numbers on separate pieces of paper stuffed inside, thumbed to a point where one felt the entire book would fall apart if picked up.

As if all these artifacts weren't personal or revealing enough, letter after letter was laid out for the public to read. Josef von Sternberg ("the man I most wanted to please"), Erich Maria Remarque, Mercedes de Costa and John Gilbert (the last two lovers shared with Greta Garbo), Jean Gabin, Yul Brynner (her code name for him being "Curly"), Douglas Fairbanks Jr., Gary Cooper, Edith Piaf, Ernest Hemingway (who always referred to her at "the Kraut"), Maurice Chevalier, Brian Aherne, Olympic tennis player Ginette Vachon, Michael Wilding, Michael Todd, and Richard Burton. ("I have had all of Elizabeth Taylor's husbands," she triumphantly and incorrectly noted.) "What's Taylor got that I haven't got?" she once demanded at a dinner party. There was no answer. "Please pass the mustard," someone asked, breaking the silence.

Public figures and politicians were represented, too: a written proposal of marriage from John D. Rockefeller, who was brusquely told, "Save another billion and I may consider it." Records of rendezvous with Ambassador Joseph P. Kennedy on the French Riviera, where they were both summering in the thirties, and later, in the White House with his son, President John F. Kennedy. ("Was I better than my father?" the latter was said to have asked as she hurriedly left the Oval Office, running late for another appointment, leaving him naked but for a towel around his waist.)

If one is to believe the content of all these letters, no one could live without her. She felt differently. "Liaison is a charming word signifying a union, not cemented and unromanticized by documents." This is how she viewed these ships-passing-in-the-night: as charming moments between the like-minded. "In Europe," she told a female passenger on a liner during one of her many transatlantic crossings, "it doesn't matter if you are a man or a woman. We make love with anybody we find attractive." The woman to whom this remark was addressed clutched her handbag to her bosom and avoided Dietrich for the rest of the journey. Perhaps this is why Marlene made the remark: she did not suffer fools gladly. A good way of getting rid of the woman.

155

In spite of her many "liaisons" over the years, her marriage to Rudolf Sieber was sacred to her. Like the Cole Porter song, she was always "true to you, darling, in my fashion." The first thing she would do whenever she arrived in Los Angeles was to go to Rudi's home in the San Fernando Valley, clean the house thoroughly, and cook him dinner. In one of his exquisitely written interviews, Rex Reed referred to her as "The Queen of Ajax," a play on her billing as "The Queen of the World."

Rudi and Marlene shared a life-long friendship. They were always there for one another, and Marlene kept both Rudi and his mentally troubled companion, Tami, in funds and comfort all their lives, even seeing to it that they were buried side by side in the Hollywood cemetery next door to Paramount Studios where she had worked.

In the pre-war years they all traveled together, often with one of Marlene's lovers, and sometimes she included her daughter. A party of five. This arrangement troubled many of her lovers, but Marlene never took their feelings into consideration. Love, lust, or passion would allow them to adjust to the unusual ménage.

Douglas Fairbanks Jr., summed it up for many who found themselves in this initially uncomfortable position: "Such a real design-for-living was quite beyond my frame of reference and I protested quietly and grumbled. But it did no good, and soon it became evident that Marlene and Rudi were indeed only technically married. They behaved like old friends. More brother and sister than husband and wife." Douglas Fairbanks Jr., stayed an entire month with this odd coupling. Marlene made it easy for them. It felt almost commonplace.

Despite the care she took with her appearance ("Makeup—too bad most of us need it") and wardrobe (a delight for designers, she would stand stock still for six hours for a fitting), she was certainly careless with her furniture—again, much of it gifts, and much of it on display in Berlin: a chest of mirrored drawers had cracks and a couple of the mirrors were missing, cigarette burns on coffee tables, chairs on insecure legs ready to topple over, chipped china, frayed carpets, and mediocre works of art. One would never have guessed these were the possessions of the most glamorous woman in the world.

A disappointing collection of cufflinks, pearl necklaces, ivory bracelets, many pendants—hardly the collection of jewelry one would expect from Dietrich. Her best pieces (among them her famed emerald cabochon bracelet) found their way to the IRS to pay disputed or neglected taxes.

It is a museum unlike any other in the world: personal to Dietrich, of interest only to film scholars and fans. At one point of our visit, six teenage girls ran along the passageways between exhibits, laughing, text-messaging, cell phones attached to their bodies like an extra appendage, showing no interest in Dietrich's memorabilia. Why had they come?

Other than seeing her onstage and exiting stage doors, it was for me the nearest I had ever come to being in her company. This was like going behind closed doors into her home.

Being alone in the museum for the most part, as Eduardo and I were, reminded me of my evening visits with Mary, years ago when I was a child. I had told her of Marlene's beauty and the enormous effect she had on me. Mary listened, but never commented. At the time I felt a touch of slight, unspoken jealousy.

In a way, I was solaced to find Dietrich's possessions in poor condition: I am also hard on my own—jam spilled on book pages, sticky finger marks around light switches. *I may well be her son, after all*, I

157

thought to myself, and the final words of her most famous song drifted into my mind: "What am I to do? I can't help it."

CHAPTER THIRTY

Influences

If the child is father to the man, I have four parents that shaped the child and therefore created the man.

It is quite obvious to me the impact Noël Coward and Marlene Dietrich have had on me: my wanderlust and love for the finest things that life can offer came from them. I have carried out Coward's dictum to always travel first class, and so far my refusal to suffer has given me a life free from major pain.

The legacy from Clive and Mary is equally obvious: their gift of allowing me to imagine whatever I wanted; permission to dream even if that dream never came true.

Before I left New Zealand for London for the first time my mother's youngest sister, my Aunt Lillian, had moved to Santa Maria, a small California city three-hours drive from Los Angeles.

Once I left London for New York and finally settled in Los Angeles, Lillian would sometimes visit Eduardo and me, and occasionally we would go to Santa Maria to spend time with her. She told me a lot about Mary, their childhood and many family matters. She was quite convinced (as was I) that Mary's time in bed was a deliberate escape from life and its troubles. "You either die or you get better, you don't spend thirty years in bed," Lillian would say.

It is not without significance that Mary had two miraculous recoveries. One enabled her to visit me in London when I was living there. She stayed six months, kept up with my round of theater going and parties, and lost her diamond shaped marquisate engagement ring, which fell down the drain when she was washing dishes.

My fondest memory of her London visit was the night I had asked her to describe childbirth to me. "Is it anything like constipation?" I asked. A reasonable question I felt, but it made her sides split with laughter. She continued to chuckle and burst out into near-uncontrollable laughter as she re-considered my question. (I never learned the answer—and to this day it still seems to me to be a reasonable question.) Oh well, just one of those mysteries of life, I guess.

Her second recovery involved another visit to me, when I lived in New York. Once again, she kept up with the parties and the theater going, made drapes for my studio apartment, co-hosted a cocktail party with me, where the guests included art collector and Listerine heiress Bunny Mellon, the Broadway star Sandy Dennis, actor Robert Loggia (whom I didn't recognize) and his wife, New York Senator Jacob Javits and his socialite wife, and Colette Harrison (Rex's first wife and mother of his son Noel). All these wives!

I had met this august group at a party where I was taken as the guest of a well-known English writer who was visiting New York at the time, and who invited me to accompany him. My fellow partygoers had no problem giving me their telephone numbers when I asked for them. I guess they assumed I must be part of their world. Each accepted my telephoned invitation for cocktails.

They arrived at my studio apartment where I served very strong martinis. Mary had made devilled eggs for them to eat. There was a lot of laughter, a lot of drinking; they stayed way beyond the time a cocktail party should end. I think they enjoyed the change from Park and Fifth Avenues parties, and perhaps appreciated my impudence in inviting them.

I never heard back from any of them, however, but in retrospect that isn't surprising. When eventually I learned the true identities of my guests, I felt just like Balzac's Cousin Bette. The poor relation!

When Mary returned to New Zealand after both these adventures, she took to her bed again. She put the brief recoveries down to prayers to Saint Anthony of Padua or Saint Jude the Obscure. I cannot remember which.

After so many years, I thought I knew my mother, or at least as well as any child could. To me, Mary led the straightforward life of a near invalid. Both of my parents were at peace with this arrangement, as was I after all that time. I was therefore sorely unprepared for Aunt Lillian's bombshell news.

"Your mother saw herself as the film actress Norma Shearer," Lillian told me.

This was startling and fascinating information: a totally new picture of my mother.

The Norma Shearer of *Marie Antoinette?*" I asked.

"No," Aunt Lillian replied. "More like the Norma Shearer of *The Women.* Your mother saw herself as a fiercely faithful wife and loving mother. She longed for a day at Elizabeth Arden's. It would have been heaven for her. Pedicures, manicures, massages. I think she lived in a dream world…" (I was astounded. "*Like me!*" I thought to myself) "where she ran everything from her bed. She loved matinee jackets and she assumed a serene pose. It would be difficult for her to be serene if she was actively involved in the raising of four children and the running of the household."

"Did you ever discuss it with her?"

"I tried a couple of times but she would feign a blinding headache and ask me to leave or stop talking," Lillian said. "I chose leaving."

I loved hearing this. Obviously Mary was a primary source of my Noël and Marlene fantasy. My mother had created a fantasy world for herself, and without telling me about it, passed on to me the need for a fantasy world of my own, the only place I ever felt truly safe, just as I believe Mary's retreat from the world around her created an air of safety for her. I wish I had learned this while she was still alive so we could have discussed it. The revelation of Mary as Norma Shearer filled me with delight.

No wonder she only half-listened to my after-dinner visits where I regaled her with stories of Marlene. Dietrich and Shearer were rivals, queens of their respective studios (Shearer at M-G-M, and Dietrich at Paramount). They had minimal contact in real life—guests at the same parties every now and then.

I am sure my source of laziness and lack of follow-through in most aspects of my life must have come from Mary, too. Both my "mothers"—Mary and Marlene had taken to their beds as a way of life. I recognize now that my bed has become been my best friend, and if I could get the conscious hours down to nine a day, I would be a happy man.

Without these four "parents"—the real ones, and the "reel" ones I would not be the person I am to day.

I don't know whether this is good or bad, but since I sort of like the person I am today, I need to thank Clive and Mary and Noël and Marlene for the life they gave me, the adventures I have experienced, the people I have met, the fun I have had, the laughter I have enjoyed, and the travel I have accomplished.

It has been an enchanted life.

Eduardo and I

BIBLIOGRAPHY

In preparing this book, the following resources were referenced and/or quoted from:

Noël Coward Bibliography

Noël by Charles Castle
Noël Coward and Radclyffe Hall: Kindred Spirits by Terry Castle
President Indicative by Noël Coward
The Uncompleted Past Unconditional by Noël Coward
Future Indefinite by Noël Coward
The Letters of Noël Coward edited by Barry Day
The Noël Coward Reader edited and with commentary by Barry Day
Noël Coward: The Complete Lyrics edited and adapted by Barry Day, Raymond Mander, and Joe Mitchenson
Noël Coward: A Biography by Clive Fisher
A Last Encore: Words by Noël Coward, Pictures from His Life and Times edited by John Hadfield
Noël Coward: A Biography by Philip Hoare
Adventures of a Gentleman's Gentleman: The Queen, Noël Coward, and I by Guy Hunting
Remembered Laughter: The Life of Noël Coward by Cole Lesley
Noël Coward and His Friends by Cole Lesley, Graham Payn, and Sheridan Morley

The Privilege of His Company: Noël Coward Remembered by William Marchant
Genius and Lust: The Creative and Sexual Lives of Cole Porter and Noël Coward by Joseph Morella and George Mazzei
A Talent to Amuse: A Biography of Noël Coward by Sheridan Morley
The Private Lives of Noël and Gertie—Two Classic Biographies in One Volume: A Talent to Amuse and A Bright Particular Star by Sheridan Morley
Theatrical Companion to Coward: A Pictorial Record of the Theatrical Works of Noël Coward by Raymond Mander, Joe Mitchenson, updated by Barry Day and Sheridan Morley
My Life With Noël Coward by raham Payn with Barry Day
The Noël Coward Diaries edited by Graham Payn and Sheridan Morley

Marlene Dietrich Bibliography

Marlene Dietrich: The Blue Angel by Steven Bach
Marlene: My Friend by David Bret
Marlene: Marlene Dietrich, A Personal Biography by Charlottle Chandler
Marlene by Marlene Dietrich (Translated from the German by Salvator Attanasio)
Dietrich: The Story of a Star by Leslie Frewin
I Wish You Love: Conversations with Marlene Dietrich by Eryk Hanut
Marlene Dietrich: An Intimate Photograph Album by Alexander Lieberman
A Woman at War: Marlene Dietrich Remembered by J. David Riva

Marlene Dietrich: Photographs and Memories, compiled by Jean-Jacques Naudet with captions by Maria Riva

Marlene Dietrich by Maria Riva

Dietrich by Malene Sheppard Skaerved

Personal Property from the Estate of Marlene Dietrich, Sotheby's Catalog

Blue Angel: The Life of Marlene Dietrich by Donald Spoto

Dietrich: A Biography by Ean Wood

ACKNOWLEDGMENTS

With over-flowing gratitude and ocean-deep affection, I wish to thank the following without whom this book would not be in your hands.

Fenella Fielding, the great British actress who read excerpts from this work at Paul Burston's Gay Literary Salon at Club Polari on April 11, 2010. She could make a grocery list sparkle. She is sheer inexplicable magic.

Raffaella De Laurentiis, the first person to encourage me to write this memoir. Martha De Laurentiis, who traveled to London to hear Fenella read my words and offer me love and encouragement. Other friends present at that reading have also earned my eternal love and gratitude. Among them: Thelma van Til, Talley Singer, Ben Crystal, and Pip Pickering.

Susan Finesman, my literary agent who told me she would find a publisher for my book within six months of reading it. And she was true to her word. Don Weise, the publisher she found for me. He was always calming to a first time author. A true gentleman.

I owe everything to my companion of thirty years, Eduardo de la Grana. He has spent half his life with me, and continues to amaze me daily with his love and laughter.

But more than anyone else, Arleen Sorkin, whose day contains twenty-six hours, for how else could she spare the time for me? She lives to comfort, inspire, to help. She eats air and invites one to partake in the feast. I always want second helpings.

ABOUT THE AUTHOR

Michael Menzies has lived all over the world, and has worked with rock 'n roll promoter Bill Graham, impresario Sol Hurok, choreographer Agnes de Mille, Broadway producer Saint-Subber, and in film with the de Laurentiis family. He now lives in Los Angeles with his companion of thirty years, Eduardo de la Grana.

Made in the USA
Lexington, KY
21 October 2013